Bridges into work?

An evaluation of Local Exchange Trading Schemes (LETS)

Colin C. Williams, Theresa Aldridge, Roger Lee, Andrew Leyshon, Nigel Thrift and Jane Tooke

The POLICY PRESS

First published in Great Britain in September 2001 by

The Policy Press
University of Bristol
34 Tyndall's Park Road
Bristol BS8 1PY
UK

Tel no +44 (0)117 954 6800
Fax no +44 (0)117 973 7308
E-mail tpp@bristol.ac.uk
www.policypress.org.uk

ISBN 1 86134 329 9

Colin C. Williams is Reader in Economic Geography and **Theresa Aldridge** is a Research Fellow, both at the University of Leicester; **Roger Lee** is Professor of Geography at Queen Mary, University of London; **Andrew Leyshon** is Professor of Economic and Social Geography at the University of Nottingham; **Nigel Thrift** is Professor of Geography at the University of Bristol; and **Jane Tooke** is Research Fellow, at Goldsmiths' College, University of London.

Cover design by Qube Design Associates, Bristol

Front cover: Photograph reproduced by kind permission of www.third-avenue.co.uk

Printed in Great Britain by Hobbs the Printers Ltd, Southampton

Contents

List of tables and figures

Tables

Figures

Acknowledgements

This research on LETS was funded by the Economic and Social Research Council (ESRC) (Ref 000237208). We are grateful to all who participated in the study, especially the coordinators and members of Stroud and Brixton LETS for their cooperation, and the many individual respondents for critical but constructive engagement.

Executive summary

Introduction

Local Exchange Trading Schemes (LETS) are non-profit making associations that use local currencies to encourage members to trade services and goods with each other. Recently, there has been considerable interest from policy makers in their potential as bridges into work for unemployed people. This report provides the first comprehensive evaluation of their effectiveness in this regard. It evaluates whether LETS are effective first, as routes into employment, second, as facilitators of self-employment and finally, at developing work beyond employment in the form of mutual aid.

Bridges into work

Building bridges into work is about more than simply moving unemployed people into formal jobs even if employment is the best route out of poverty. Given the problems of achieving and sustaining full employment and the desire of people to rebuild community spirit in their localities, initiatives such as LETS need to be considered not only as a means of facilitating entry into formal employment but also as capacity building vehicles that develop social capital in the form of reciprocity. As such, LETS are here evaluated in terms of their effectiveness at both improving employability and facilitating engagement in another form of work, namely mutual aid.

Geographies of LETS

Introducing LETS

In the UK, the first LETS was founded in Norwich in 1985. By early 1992 there were just five LETS in operation in the UK, rising to 40 a year later and to 200 by 1994. In 1999, 303 LETS were found to be operating in the UK.

Four inter-connecting methods were used to evaluate the effectiveness of LETS both at helping members into formal employment and as tools for facilitating mutual aid. First, a postal survey of all LETS coordinators was undertaken in 1999. Of the 303 LETS identified and surveyed, 113 responded (37%). Second, a membership survey was conducted with 2,515 postal questionnaires being sent out and 810 (34%) returned. Third, in-depth action-orientated ethnographic research was carried out during eight-month periods with two LETS in contrasting locations: the semi-rural area of Stroud and the deprived urban area of Brixton in London. Finally, key figures in UK LETS development were interviewed to gain an understanding of current circumstances in UK LETS, examples of good practice, and views on their future.

UK LETS have an average of 72 members and a mean turnover equivalent to £4,664. Extrapolating from this, the total UK LETS membership can be estimated to be 21,816 and the total turnover equivalent to £1.4 million. In terms of their material value, therefore, these schemes are relatively insignificant compared with the wider economy. However, as with any economic system, their wider social contribution cannot be reduced to flows of material value.

Most LETS are founded for non-economic reasons. The results from the survey of LETS coordinators also indicate that many LETS established as a means of building an alternative economy soon changed their rationale once they became operational. In all these cases, it was community-building rationales that became more prominent and this was often linked to a change of personnel. Men who set up LETS had more ideological rationales (for example, developing an 'alternative' to capitalism) while the reasons for women founding LETS were nearly wholly grounded in practical community-building motives. Over time, however, men tended to drop out of their 'leadership' role (often as they became disillusioned) and the women took over with their more practical community-centred rationales.

Mapping UK LETS

Given that LETS currently cover just 16% of the land area of the UK, a principal barrier to participation is that LETS do not exist in many localities. The geographical distribution of LETS, moreover, is uneven. They tend to be skewed towards affluent southern regions of the UK. In part, this is because the higher cost of living in these areas means that low-income groups have a greater need for additional coping mechanisms and, in part, it is due to the greater concentration of 'green' or 'alternative' population groups in these regions.

LETS membership

LETS are joined predominantly by low-income groups who are either not employed or are self-employed, by women, and by those aged 30-59. Indeed, if non-employment and low household incomes are taken as surrogate indicators of social exclusion, membership is heavily skewed towards socially excluded groups. A total of 62% of members are not employed and 66% live in households with a gross income of less than £20,000. Members are, however, largely from a very particular group of the 'socially excluded'. They tend to be well educated, to have few kinship networks in the locality and to be 'green' in political orientation. Indeed, in some cases, their 'exclusion' from mainstream employment appears to be due to disenchantment with formal employment and a desire to build alternative forms of work and welfare. Thus, in terms of why people join:

- 25% do so for ideological purposes – LETS for them are 'expressive communities', acts of political protest and resistance to the 'mainstream' where ideals can be put into practice;
- 3% join explicitly to improve their employability and these are nearly all people seeking self-employment;
- 23% see LETS as a 'social' vehicle either for building communities, meeting people or helping others;
- 42% view LETS as an 'economic' vehicle for exchanging goods and services (20%), overcoming their lack of money (12%), receiving a specific service (9%) and using skills (1%).

'Social'/community-building reasons for joining LETS tend to be cited by employed people and relatively affluent and economic reasons by the relatively poor and unemployed people.

LETS as bridges into work

LETS as routes into employment

To evaluate LETS in this regard, the study examined the number of formal jobs created through them, their ability to facilitate the acquisition and maintenance of skills, whether they provide a test bed for new potential formal businesses and their ability to develop self-esteem and to maintain the employment ethic. Our findings were:

- only a dozen or so formal jobs have been directly created by the 303 LETS;
- however, 5% of respondents said LETS had directly helped them gain formal employment: working in the LETS office administering the scheme had enabled valuable administrative skills to be acquired which had been used successfully to apply for formal jobs;
- 27% of all respondents asserted that participating in LETS had boosted their self-confidence (33% of the registered unemployed people);
- 15% had acquired new skills through LETS (24% of the registered unemployed people), mostly related to computing, administration and interpersonal skills.

LETS as facilitators of self-employment

- A total of 11% of members asserted that LETS had provided them with a useful seed-bed for developing self-employed business ventures.
- LETS had enabled them to develop their client base (cited by 41% of those who were self-employed), ease the cash-flow of their business (cited by 29%) and provide a test bed for their products and services (cited by nearly all who defined themselves as self-employed).

In consequence, although LETS do not create many jobs directly, they do provide a useful springboard into employment and self-employment for a small but significant proportion of members.

LETS as vehicles for mutual aid

- A total of 76% of respondents asserted that LETS had helped them to develop a network of people on whom they could call for help while 56% stated that they had helped them develop a wider network of friends and 31% deeper friendships. LETS, therefore, develop 'bridges' (that is, bringing people together who did not previously know each other) more than 'bonds' (that is, bringing people who already know each other closer together). They develop the 'strength of weak ties'.
- For two thirds (65%) of registered unemployed people, LETS had helped them cope with unemployment, with 3% of their total income coming from their LETS activity.
- 40% of members (but 62% of registered unemployed people and 51% of low-income households) assert that LETS provided them with access to interest-free credit.

LETS are thus widely seen by members as an effective vehicle for developing means of livelihood beyond employment. Why, therefore, have so few people joined LETS?

Barriers to participation in LETS

Barriers to joining LETS

- Research with non-members in Brixton and Stroud highlighted that 93% and 51% respectively had not heard about LETS.

- When the concept and practical details of joining LETS were discussed with groups of non-members, they tended to ask 'Is this novel idea credible? Is it for me? What will I get out of it? What are the costs of involvement? What have I got to offer?'. The resultant weighing-up process involved non-members balancing the resources that they would have to commit (including time and energy) with the rewards they might receive from participation. Many expressed that, on balance, joining was too much of a risk.

Barriers to increased trading on LETS

Three principal barriers to increased trading on LETS were identified:

- the organisational capacity of LETS, including their reliance on a limited number of volunteers to run them who suffer 'burnout', and the difficulties in maintaining up-to-date information;
- fears about negotiating trades, including worries about skill identification, pricing and the quality of the product;
- the small size of LETS which often results in a narrow and limited range of goods and services on offer.

Strategies for LETS development

To tackle these barriers to participation in LETS, we argue that changes are required not only in the internal operating environment of individual LETS but also in their external operating environment. For LETS to open themselves to a broader range of the population:

- marketing is required to inform a wider range of people of their existence;
- people need to perceive LETS as something for them;
- people need to see that they can make a contribution.

Achieving these changes requires small-scale funding in order to enable LETS to develop effective marketing channels, raise awareness of trading possibilities and to work with targeted groups to encourage their involvement. However, the very act of formalising support immediately undermines the independence and autonomy of LETS which, for many, is their main attractive and significant characteristic. Nevertheless, to concentrate on making individual LETS more organisationally effective is a necessary but insufficient solution.

To become more effective as bridges into work for unemployed people, changes are also required in the external operating environment of LETS. On the one hand, the institutional thinness of LETS both at the regional and national level needs to be tackled. At present, few regional networks exist and there is a void at the national level with no funded 'one-stop-shop' either for answering queries, developing best practice or for providing support to those interested in LETS development. On the other hand, there is a need for much greater clarity by central government over how LETS earnings are to be treated, especially with regard to registered unemployed people, taxation and social security benefits. Without such increased certainties, unemployed people will continue to conclude that joining LETS is too much of a risk.

Conclusions

In the current era of employment-centred social policy, policy makers have focused on LETS as a way to create jobs and to improve employability. This report, however, reveals that their major contribution is as a facilitator of mutual aid. As a tool for achieving 'full employment', LETS are relatively ineffective. However, as a vehicle for facilitating 'full-engagement', LETS have much greater utility.

As such, there is much to learn from LETS. Rather than rely on formal employment as the sole route out of poverty, the members of these pioneering initiatives are adopting a 'work ethic' rather than an 'employment ethic' in order to alleviate their situation. Participants are using LETS as reciprocal exchange networks to construct alternative means of livelihood. Policy, therefore, needs to follow suit. By harnessing LETS as a tool for not only creating jobs and improving employability but also harnessing mutual aid, the full potential of such initiatives could start to be realised. Moreover, by recognising and valuing mutual aid, policy would be taking the first

step to recognising that basic material needs and creative desires may be met just as well by pursuing 'full engagement' rather than full employment.

Introduction

Talk to anybody in the contemporary UK. Ask them if they know about any work that needs to be undertaken. Once they get started, they will doubtless present you with a very long list of tasks. Then ask them why this work is not being undertaken. After all, there are many people who, for a multitude of different reasons, would like to do some of this work. One of the main reasons they will give you is that there is a lack of money to pay for it. Put another way, demand and supply cannot come together because of the scarcity of money. But money is a social construct and a novel solution to this problem has swept across the UK over the past decade or so. People are deciding that if money, as a scarce commodity, is constraining exchange, the way to overcome it is by creating new forms of currency.

These local currencies that have been springing up to bring people who need work doing together with those who wish to make an active contribution to their communities are the subject matter of this report. Akin to the 'baby-sitting circle' that uses matchsticks as a unit of currency to pay for childcare undertaken, Local Exchange and Trading Schemes (LETS) create a unit of currency, but do so in order that people can undertake a much wider range of tasks for each other. LETS are private formal associations for pursuing economically orientated collective self-help based on not-for-profit and cooperative principles.

Establishing a LETS is a relatively simple task. A group of people gets together and decides to create a unit of exchange (for example, acorns in Totnes, strouds in Stroud, readies in Reading, favours in Calderdale). In order to offer goods and services to each other priced in these units, each member makes a list offering various types of work, along with a list of requests of what s/he wants doing. These are then entered into a directory that is regularly published and circulated to all members, in a similar form to 'Yellow Pages'. Individuals can then decide what they want to trade, who they want to trade with and how much trading they wish to do. The price for each transaction is arrived at through agreement between the buyer and seller. The LETS keeps a record of these transactions by a system of cheques that are written in the local currency. Each time a piece of work is undertaken, the person who has sold the goods and/or service sends the cheque that s/he has received to the treasurer. The treasurer acts in a similar manner to a bank in that s/he sends out regular statements of account to members. No cash is issued. All transactions are by cheque and are written in the local currency.

The level of LETS units exchanged is thus entirely dependent on the extent of trading undertaken. Money in LETS arises from exchange as well as acting as a means of exchange (Lietaer, 2001). This money does not need to be earned before it can be spent. Credit is freely available and interest-free.

The benefits of LETS can be seen in the following quotes from an unemployed single woman in her early fifties:

"The reason I'm in LETS is because I have very little money and because I very much want to be part of the community as well. If I was wealthy then it would probably not be the first thing I think of, but because I am very limited with my financial resources, really the LETS system is the first possibility I think of when I need things done. I think more in LETS than I do in money in a way, because I

have little money and because it's a wonderful possibility to do all of the things I wouldn't otherwise be able to do."

This woman has purchased alternative therapies and paid for them in local currency. For her, this was not some quirky luxury but a necessity. As she puts it,

"Without the acupuncture, I would be back to where I was two years ago, only being able to stand up for five minutes at a time. The LETS has been a lifeline for me in many ways. It is the only means I have of getting access to such therapy. I don't have the money to pay £30-40 an hour outside the LETS."

LETS has provided a solution to her healthcare problems. It has also gone someway to solving her transport problems. Living in a relatively isolated rural area with what she describes as "appalling public transport", she has been able to pay for lifts into town both to attend her therapy sessions and do her grocery shopping.

However, LETS are not just about what you can receive. LETS are also important in terms of their ability to provide 'bridges into work'. Indeed, it is the multitude of ways in which LETS do this which is the subject of this report. Our aim is to evaluate critically the effectiveness of LETS in this regard. This is an important issue. Recent years have seen a great deal of interest by policy makers in the potential of LETS as bridges into work for the unemployed both at the national level (for example, DETR, 1998, 1999; DfEE, 1999; Home Office, 1999; SEU, 2000) and by regional and local government. Until now, however, there has been little evidence available on whether or not LETS are effective. Most previous studies have been one-off investigations of individual LETS and have frequently not considered their role in increasing the accessibility of work for the unemployed. Instead, they have focused on LETS as a new type of moral economy (see for example, Lee, 1996), a response to globalisation (see for example, Pacione, 1997a, 1997b, 1997c; Tibbett, 1997; Hart, 2000), a tool for promoting 'green' politics or sustainable development (see for example, Seyfang, 1998; Barry and Proops, 2000; Fitzpatrick and Caldwell, 2001: forthcoming) or as a new social movement (see for example, North, 1996, 1998, 1999; Purdue et al, 1997; O'Doherty et al, 1999). Thus, in this report, we build on the few one-off studies of individual LETS that have focused on these schemes

as routes into work for the unemployed (for example, Barnes et al, 1996; Williams, 1996a, 1996b, 1996c).

To facilitate 'evidence-based policy making', we report the results of the first comprehensive national study of the effectiveness of LETS as bridges into work. Undertaken between 1997 and 2000, this comprised three main stages. First, a comprehensive survey was undertaken using a 'snow-balling' technique to identify all known LETS in the UK, followed by a postal questionnaire of all LETS coordinators to identify the magnitude and character of these schemes. A full membership survey of 26 LETS chosen using a maximum variation sampling technique was then undertaken. Second, in-depth action-oriented ethnographic research was conducted in two contrasting localities – the deprived inner London borough of Brixton and the rural town of Stroud. This research involved continuous residence in the two localities over an eight-month period and close involvement in the day-to-day functioning of the two LETS. This close involvement enabled interviews and focus groups with members and non-members, as well as reflexive action research that provided a more detailed understanding of whether and how LETS act as routes into work for the unemployed and other social groups. Third, key figures in the UK LETS development were interviewed to gain an understanding not only of current developments and good practice but controversies and debates.

This report presents some of the findings and is organised as follows. Part One sets out the contrasting meanings of 'bridges into work'. Chapter 2 introduces its mainstream meaning as the development of initiatives to insert people into formal employment. Chapter 3 argues that constructing routes into work is about more than simply moving the unemployed into formal jobs even if employment is the best route out of poverty. It concludes that initiatives such as LETS need to be considered not only as a means of facilitating entry into formal employment but also as capacity-building vehicles that develop additional means of livelihood beyond formal employment.

Part Two provides an overview of the anatomy of LETS to enable their evaluation as a means of both improving employability and harnessing the capacity of populations to engage in mutual aid. Chapter 4 examines the origins and growth of LETS in the UK, the methods used in this research, and an exploration of why LETS are created, how they are promoted and their current trading levels. Chapter 5 moves on to map UK LETS and explores their uneven spatial distribution in the UK. Finally, Chapter 6 examines the membership of LETS and members' motivations for joining.

Part Three evaluates the extent to which LETS enable access to work for the unemployed. Three contrasting processes are evaluated:

- the effectiveness of LETS as routes into employment (Chapter 7);
- the effectiveness of LETS as seed-beds for developing self-employed business ventures (Chapter 8);
- the effectiveness of LETS in creating reciprocal exchange networks (Chapter 9).

Our finding is that although LETS indirectly provide routes into employment by improving employability and are effective as seed-beds for the development of self-employed business ventures, they are most effective at creating livelihoods beyond employment. However, significant barriers prevent a wider range of the unemployed from joining and participating in LETS. These barriers are outlined in Chapters 10 and 11, while Chapter 12 explores the changes required in LETS at the local, regional and national levels to tackle these barriers. Chapter 13 provides a concluding evaluation of LETS as bridges into work.

Part One

Bridges into work

Routes into employment

Building bridges into work for the unemployed is often narrowly conceptualised to mean creating routes into formal employment. Based on the view that employment is the best route out of poverty, an employment-centred social policy agenda has emerged that equates social inclusion with insertion into employment and social exclusion with unemployment. In this chapter, we first set out the various policies inspired by this approach to build bridges into employment and, second, unpack how LETS are viewed in this approach.

The 'making employment pay' approach

Since the election of New Labour in 1997, a concerted effort has been made to pursue policy interventions that deal with unemployment in general and the plight of jobless households in particular. Recognising the increasing polarisation of households into those with multiple earners and those with no earners (Pinch, 1993; Williams and Windebank, 1995; Gregg and Wadsworth, 1996; Dunford, 1997), the UK government has formulated work and welfare policies to make work (that is, employment) pay. The intention has been to ensure that when the unemployed and jobless households move from benefits to work, they should be financially better off as a result (HM Treasury, 1997, 1998; DSS, 1999).

This has involved the introduction of numerous 'activation' policies. The underlying basis of this reform programme is the belief that the welfare state no longer functions effectively and requires extensive modernisation to meet the needs of today's society. At the forefront of this modernisation process is the theme of employment-centred social policy, with the prime objective of getting the unemployed back into formal jobs and away from dependency on welfare benefits. The central ethos is to enhance the incentives for individuals to move from welfare into work. In this context, social policy reforms have centred on two key areas: first, reducing the poverty and unemployment traps by improving work incentives, and second, improving the employability of those people who are unemployed. The policies that constitute this 'employment first' approach fall into three broad categories:

- *Reforming welfare benefits under the welfare to work programmes:* this has targeted specific unemployed groups such as lone parents, the young, the long-term unemployed and people with disabilities.
- *Modernising the tax and benefits system:* this includes, for example, the Working Families' Tax and Childcare Tax Credits, alterations to National Insurance contributions and introducing a 10 pence starting rate of tax.
- *Improving conditions within employment:* including the Minimum Wage, implementation of European Union Employment Directives, and the Fairness at Work programme.

Many of these policy initiatives to facilitate entry into employment are positive incentives to 'make employment pay'. For example, the Working Families Tax Credit (WFTC), introduced in October 1999 to replace the previous system of Family Credit, allows people with children who work 16 hours or over to claim WFTC and its accompanying Childcare Tax Credit, which are more generous than the previous system of Family Credit. The new tax credits reform the tax and benefits system in a manner that distinguishes between in-work and unemployment benefits. For example, they are paid through the wage packet and not the 'Giro', and administered by the Inland Revenue rather than the Benefits Agency. The intention is to encourage the unemployed to take low hours or low-paid jobs and to lessen child poverty by redistributing income to low-income families who participate in paid employment. There is also a wider desire to use this as a basis for creating a fully integrated tax-benefit system in the distant future. The WFTC, alongside the National Childcare Strategy and the extension of benefit claims and work obligations to both members of unemployed couples (whose children are over 16 years old), thus constitute a new strategy for tacking unemployment in the UK. These are all positive measures designed to encourage the take-up of paid employment as a solution to social exclusion.

At the same time, however, there are also 'sticks' or negative incentives to encourage entry into employment. The principal mechanism used to improve employability and address the propensity of the benefits system to entrap claimants into a life on benefits is the New Deal programme. This programme is a prime example of the Labour government's approach to 'active welfare policies' (HM Treasury, 1997, 1998; Bennett and Walker, 1998; Hills, 1998; Oppenheim, 1998; Gregg et al, 1999; Powell, 1999). In 1998-99, the New Deals for young people, the long-term unemployed, lone parents and people with long-term sickness and disabilities were launched. For groups such as the long-term unemployed and the young unemployed, participation in the New Deal scheme is compulsory and non-compliance is subject to benefit suspension or fines. For the first four months of the New Deal, participants take part in the Gateway – an advisory period designed to help them select the most appropriate option from the five choices of subsidised work, voluntary work, vocational training, education or self-employment. Wage and training subsidies are paid to employers, training organisations and so on. These schemes thus contain strong elements of compulsion, but they also provide a broader structure of opportunities than were available under the previous government.

In consequence, there are now numerous activation policies in the armoury of government. However, as many have started to point out (for example, Lister, 1997; Levitas, 1998), the weapons being stockpiled in this armoury are designed to eliminate only one specific type of enemy: those not engaged in employment. Defining inclusion as employment and exclusion as unemployment, the responses are designed solely to exterminate this one foe. While it would be fruitless to deny that this form of inactivity is, in most cases, a principal basis of social exclusion, it is nonetheless important to recognise that there are other types of informal inactivity that also lead to social exclusion. At present little attention is paid to these informal forms of inactivity. On the rare occasions that they are considered, participation in work beyond employment is largely seen to be part of a separate 'social' agenda which is subservient to the core 'economic' agenda that seeks only one specific type of activation: participation in formal employment.

The role of LETS as routes into employment

What is the role of LETS in this employment-focused approach? To answer this, it is first necessary to understand that LETS are seen as part of the third sector. LETS conform to all of the criteria usually used to define the third sector: they are private formal associations for pursuing economically orientated collective self-help based on not-for-profit and cooperative principles (see for example, Catterall et al, 1996; Amin et al, 1999). In an employment-centred policy approach, this third sector is predominantly conceptualised in terms of its ability to generate jobs and improve the employability of those who are unemployed (CDF, 1995; Fordham, 1995; European Commission, 1996, 1997, 1998; OECD, 1996; ECOTEC, 1998; Archibugi, 2000).

Consequently, the key issue from this perspective is whether LETS are capable either of providing a new means of employment creation to complement the efforts of the public and private sectors, or of improving the employability of the unemployed. With regard to the former, the perception is that, in an age of structural unemployment and growing restrictions on the reach of the market and state, the private and public sectors can no longer be relied on to create sufficient jobs (Amin et al, 1999). The de-coupling of productivity increases from employment growth in the private sector and the supposed adverse effects of state spending on international competitiveness mean that the postwar corporatist welfare state model is no longer sustainable. The 'fiscal crisis of the state' widely predicted in the 1970s (see for example, O'Connor, 1973; Habermas, 1975) has come to fruition insofar as increasingly globalised financial markets constrain the fiscal and monetary policies of national governments. In this context, third sector initiatives such as LETS are viewed as a potential solution. They are thus bolted onto conventional job creation programmes and policies either as an additional means by which employment can be created beyond the public and private sectors or as a means of providing people with a springboard to enter formal employment. This conceptualisation of the role of the third sector is not unique to the UK. It is perceived in the same vein throughout both mainland Europe and North America (Mayer and Katz, 1985; OECD, 1995; European Commission, 1996, 1998; World Bank, 1997). As evidence, one has only to note that the European Commission's major mechanism to stimulate the third sector is entitled the 'Third system and employment' (see ECOTEC, 1998; Haughton, 1998; Westerdahl and Westlund, 1998).

In consequence, this approach views the development of third sector initiatives as complementing the current range of carrots and sticks used under the umbrella term of 'making work pay' that seeks to increase the numbers available for employment. It complements these policies in two ways. On the one hand, it provides additional job opportunities to those created by the public and private sectors for those spirited into the labour market. On the other hand, it improves employability by enabling those excluded from the public and private sectors to maintain and enhance their job-related skills. In this sense, the third sector is an essential supplement to the current 'making employment pay' policy agenda. A job requires not only a person to be available but also a job opportunity and a suitably qualified person. The role of the third sector is to provide these additional job opportunities and to improve employability by helping people to maintain and acquire skills, and to develop self-confidence and self-esteem.

Evaluating LETS as routes into employment

In this context, the effectiveness of an initiative such as LETS is measured by whether they create jobs and improve employability. On the first issue of creating jobs, the evaluation criterion is quite simply the number of formal jobs created by such an initiative. On the second issue of improving employability, the evaluation criteria used will assess the ability of LETS to facilitate skill acquisition and maintenance so as to improve employability, and whether they provide a test bed for potential formal businesses to facilitate self-employment. Finally, intangible aspects of employability will need to be evaluated – predominantly whether LETS develop self-esteem and maintain an employment ethic.

Conclusions

In an employment-focused approach, the third sector is conceptualised predominantly in terms of its ability to generate jobs and improve the employability of those who are unemployed. As such, the key issues for LETS in this analysis are whether they can provide either a new means of employment creation to complement the efforts of the public and private sectors, or improve employability. Evaluation criteria include the number of formal jobs created, whether they facilitate the acquisition and maintenance of skills, whether they provide the self-employed with a test bed for new formal businesses and whether they develop self-esteem and maintain an employment ethic. For some, however, the idea that building bridges into work is solely about creating routes into formal employment has been heavily criticised. For these analysts, to deliberate on 'work' and 'inclusion' is, as is shown in the following chapter, to discuss more than inserting the unemployed into formal employment.

3

Constructing alternative means of livelihood

In recent years, a number of critics have questioned whether 'activation' policies should be so narrowly conceptualised as is the case in the 'making employment pay' approach (see, for example, Macfarlane, 1996; Levitas, 1998; Lister, 1997; Beck, 2000). In this chapter, we contribute to this line of argument. Our thesis is that building bridges into work for the unemployed is about more than simply moving the unemployed into formal jobs – even if employment remains the best route out of poverty. Inclusion is about more than formal employment, and third sector initiatives such as LETS need to be considered not only as a means of enabling people to enter employment but also as capacity-building vehicles that develop additional means of livelihood beyond job creation. Consequently, there is a need to evaluate LETS in terms of their effectiveness in improving employability and in harnessing the capacity of populations to engage in reciprocal exchange networks and under socially reproductive activity.

Therefore, we first provide some rationales for extending the notion of 'building bridges into work' beyond the narrow idea of moving the unemployed into formal jobs. Following this, we outline a conceptualisation of LETS grounded in a wider view of what is meant both by inclusion/exclusion and by 'the economic'.

Rationales for conceptualising 'bridges into work' as more than insertion into formal jobs

At present, social policy assumes that employment is the 'royal road' to combating exclusion and promoting inclusion. Thus, active social policies look almost exclusively at paid employment when it comes to establishing inclusion. However, for a small but growing number of analysts the multi-dimensionality of exclusion and inclusion means that social inclusion cannot be equated with insertion into the subsystem of formal employment, even if this remains the best route out of poverty (see for example, Macfarlane, 1996; Levitas, 1998; Lister, 1997; Beck, 2000; Williams and Windebank, 2001a).

To put all of one's eggs into the policy basket of creating sufficient formal jobs is a precarious strategy. Alternative means of livelihood in other subsystems of work also need to be developed as complementary social inclusion policies in order to diversify people's options and, therefore, reduce the chances of failure. Indeed, there are good reasons why active social policies need to broaden their scope. These relate, first, to the current inequalities in the ability of people to participate not only in employment but also in other subsystems of economic activity and, second, to the niggling doubt in many people's minds that full employment can be (or should be) achieved and maintained.

Participation in work beyond employment

It is sometimes assumed that many of those excluded from employment compensate for this exclusion by participating more heavily in other forms of work such as mutual aid (Gutmann, 1978; Rosanvallon, 1980; Matthews, 1983; Button, 1984). Indeed, this notion that the informal sector acts as a substitute for employment on an individual and household basis often results in the adoption of a laissez-faire regulatory approach towards such work. Such benign neglect is thus seen to be in the interests of those excluded from employment. In recent decades, however, a large number of empirical studies throughout the advanced economies have critically evaluated a 'marginality thesis'. This states that participation in informal work is greater among marginalised populations, who conduct such activity as an economic survival strategy.

In the UK, for example, it is now well understood (at least in academic circles) that adopting a laissez-faire approach towards the informal sphere reinforces, rather than reduces, the social inequalities produced by inclusion in and exclusion from formal employment. In fact, numerous studies reveal that unemployed people and jobless households engage in less self-provisioning, less unpaid community work and less paid informal work than employed individuals and households in which people are in formal jobs (Pahl, 1984; Leonard, 1998; Williams and Windebank, 1999, 2000, 2001a, 2001b; Williams et al, 2001).

It can no longer be assumed that those marginalised or excluded from the subsystem of formal employment compensate for their exclusion from this realm by their inclusion in the informal subsystems of work. Let us take just one example. It is often believed that rural populations engage in higher amounts of unpaid community exchange than urban populations. A recent study in rural England explores this issue (Williams et al, 2001). It reveals that, although unpaid community exchange *is* slightly higher among rural populations, it tends to be relatively affluent households in jobs who both give and receive the vast majority of this unpaid community exchange. Jobless rural households find themselves not only excluded from employment but also from the social support networks that might ameliorate their livelihood. Similar findings have been identified in urban areas (Williams and Windebank, 2001b).

How this exclusion from spheres of participation beyond employment can be tackled is an important issue for social policy, not least due to the recent concerns that social capital (that is, networks of trust and reciprocity) may be dwindling (Putnam, 2000). Given that the empirical evidence shows how those excluded from employment are unable to compensate for their exclusion by participating in the informal

sphere, there is need to consider the case for parallel interventions in this informal realm. To pursue active formal labour market policies is to deal with only one side of the equation. Similar inclusion policies are also required to integrate these groups into other subsystems of work.

The unemployed do not participate in informal economic activity because they lack the following:

- money and access to equipment (that is, economic capital);
- people on whom they can call for help, especially when made unemployed (that is, social network capital);
- skills, confidence or the physical abilities to conduct such activities (that is, human capital); and
- trust that, even if they engage in mutual aid for others, they would not be reported to the authorities. This is especially significant among the unemployed (Pahl, 1984; Thomas, 1992; Williams and Windebank, 2001b).

The suggestion, therefore, is that if these barriers to participation among the unemployed could be tackled, there would be an opportunity for the current inequalities in reciprocal exchange to be resolved. This issue is discussed in Chapter 9.

Consequently, just as activation policies are required to facilitate insertion into the subsystem of employment and policy intervention is needed to reduce the inequalities in the labour market, the same applies to other subsystems of work. In order to construct alternative means of livelihood in these informal subsystems, complementary social inclusion policies (CSIPs) are required to overcome barriers to participation in the informal sphere, alongside initiatives to insert the unemployed into employment. Without CSIPs, unemployed people and jobless households will not only remain excluded from these alternative coping practices as well as employment, but the multi-dimensionality of social exclusion and inclusion will not be addressed. However, it is not only the current inequalities in participation in these other subsystems of work that provide a rationale for defining 'building bridges into work' as something more than insertion into formal jobs.

The feasibility of full employment

The second rationale for pursuing a broader definition relates to the feasibility and desirability of an almost exclusive emphasis on a policy of full formal employment.

Is full employment feasible? In the present era so dominated by the ideology of full employment, such a question is seldom asked. Indeed, even to ask it is to risk being classified as some sort of heretic or crank. The future of work in contemporary discourse is not open. Only one possible future is discussed and it is the future of full employment. And to listen to current party political discourses, the achievement of this future is nearly upon us. However, the stark reality is that, in the UK in May 2000, despite one of the highest ever employment participation rates being achieved, just 74.4% of the working-age population were in employment. One in four people of working age were not. Put another way, some 9 million of the working-age population were without jobs (Williams and Windebank, 2001b). The jobs gap between the current level of employment and the full employment of the working-age population is very wide.

At this point, some might argue that many of those without jobs are the early retired or those with spouses in well-paid employment and should therefore be left out of the equation. If this is so, little needs to be done. The problem, however, is that this is not the case. The decline of the single-earner household, traditionally a male breadwinner household, has resulted in an increasing polarisation of households into those in which all are jobless and those in which all are in employment (Williams and Windebank, 1995; Gregg and Wadsworth, 1996). Indeed, between 1983 and 1994, while the proportion of households with some people in employment and some without fell from 30.1% to 18.6%, the proportion of households in which all were jobless grew from 16.0% to 18.9% and the share of those in which all were in employment rose from 53.9% to 62.1% (Gregg and Wadsworth, 1996). Far from the non-employed or 'economically inactive' being the spouses of employed people, the working-age jobless are concentrated in households where all are jobless. This means not only that the jobs gap is far greater than suggested by official unemployment figures but that the non-employed (who are often not counted in official unemployment figures) can no longer be ignored.

The issue that needs to be considered, therefore, is whether sufficient jobs can be created to achieve full employment. Evidence from the UK labour market is far from clear. It is, therefore, logical not to rely solely on this policy. Instead, it is necessary to consider how job creation can be complemented by additional initiatives to provide alternative routes out of poverty.

The desirability of full employment

Besides the questions surrounding the feasibility of full employment, there are also more normative questions surrounding the pursuit of full employment. Throughout the advanced economies, a deep division appears to have emerged between government policy and individual attitudes. In policy-making circles, the desire appears to be to make employment the central focus of people's lives. Indeed, many on the Left who once bemoaned the exploitation inherent in employer–employee relationships are now among the principal advocates of getting employees into this relationship.

However, at the very time that the 'employment ethic' has taken centre stage in policy making, it is evident that many individuals have started to redefine the importance of employment in their lives. There is now a range of accounts that indicate how people are placing less emphasis on the importance of employment and are seeking more of a work–life balance (Zoll, 1989; Coupland, 1991; Cannon, 1994; Gorz, 1999).

These studies reveal a marked de-centring of the idea about the growing involvement and identification of the whole person with his/her job. This disaffection with employment is spreading in all countries and throughout a cross-section of the entire working population, however obsessive the concern with income and the fear of losing one's job. Among western Europeans aged between 16 and 34, 'work' or 'career' have been shown to trail far behind five other priorities in a list of "things which are really important to you personally" (Yankelovich, 1995). The five priorities found in Yakelovich's study are: having friends (95%); having enough free time (80%); being in good physical health (77%); spending time with one's family (74%); and having an active social life (74%). Only 9% of those questioned (and 7% of young people between the ages of 13 and 25) cited work as "the main factor for success in life". Similarly, in the UK, some 57% of people aged between 18 and 30 "refuse to let work interfere with their lives", compared to only 37% of those aged between 45 and 54 (cited in Pahl, 1995). In a sample of upper-middle class full-time employees in the US, Schor (1995) found that 73% take the view they would have a better quality of life if they worked less, spent less and had more time for themselves. Indeed, some 28% of those questioned had chosen to 'downshift' (that is, voluntarily earn and spend less) in order to lead a more meaningful life.

It appears that a cultural transition has taken place and that the political world has not caught up with it. Generally, people are in employment because the danger is that, if they lose it, they will lose their income and all the opportunities for activity and contact with others. Employment is thus valued, not for the satisfaction that work itself brings, but for the rights and entitlements attached to employment and employment alone (Gorz, 1999, p 64). While citizens' rights remain confined to employment rights, as displayed by the watering down of citizens' rights to those of workers' (that is, employees') rights in the European Union, this situation seems likely to continue.

In sum, although it is often taken for granted in policy making that people want a formal job, it is usually the *income from the job* and the rights arising from it, *rather than the job itself* that people desire. This raises the spectre that, despite the centring of employment in economic and social policy, attitudes towards employment are shifting in the opposite direction. There needs, therefore, to be a reconsideration of whether this 'employment ethic' should remain at the heart of economic and social policy. Just as people are recognising and valuing work beyond employment, there is a case for economic and social policy following suit.

Role of LETS as an alternative means of livelihood

Considering these arguments for defining 'bridges into work' more broadly to include forms of

participation beyond employment, the role of LETS in the future of work and welfare is cast in a very different light. Rather than viewing these third sector initiatives as part of a strategy to achieve 'full employment', this perspective interprets their principal role to be one of facilitating 'full engagement'. By 'full engagement' is meant a situation in which all citizens who are able can engage in work (either formal or informal work) in order to meet their basic material needs and creative desires (see Mayo, 1996; Jordan et al, 2000; Williams and Windebank, 2000). As such, the role of LETS is not just to create jobs and improve employability, but also to facilitate reciprocal exchange. At the heart of this approach is an understanding of the need to reduce the importance attached to conventional employment and recognise people's broader social contributions by valuing the vast and growing amount of work outside employment that takes place in society (cf, Lister, 1997; Levitas, 1998). This perhaps signifies a return to moral economy (Lee, 1996).

However, there is also an understanding that "unless the laissez-faire approach towards such work is transcended and pro-active policies developed, the exploitation and socio-economic inequalities inherent in such work will continue to prevail" (Williams and Windebank, 2000, p 365). Given that those excluded from employment are also the people least able to draw on alternative means of livelihood, there is a need for instruments that can improve what Sen (1998) calls the 'capabilities' of people to help themselves. As a form of locally constructed and negotiated economy, LETS may provide access to opportunities for reciprocity and so stem the degradation of the social fabric in terms of the capability for reciprocal exchange (Macfarlane, 1996; OECD, 1996; Chanan, 1999; Putnam, 2000).

In this context, it is necessary to draw a clear distinction between two very different forms of LETS. *LETSystems* are highly ambitious circuits of social reproduction based on the aim of providing multiple forms of currency through which to engage in exchange and hence to link production and consumption in a variety of ways, unconstrained by singular, 'official' forms of currency. However, notwithstanding their potentially radical and fundamental impact as a challenge to singular currencies, they are as yet relatively underdeveloped in practical terms. By contrast, *LETS schemes* have more modest ambitions to supplement 'official' currencies on a local basis and so to offer alternative circuits of social reproduction to their members. In this report, it is the 'alternatives' provided by LETS schemes that are the focus of attention.

Evaluating LETS as enablers of alternative means of livelihood

To evaluate the potential of LETS to provide alternative means of livelihood or social reproduction, a range of indicators is employed. Besides those that indicate the ability of LETS to act as a means of creating jobs and improving employability, LETS are also evaluated in terms of their ability to tackle the barriers to participation in reciprocal exchange. This relative inability of the unemployed and low-income groups to engage in mutual aid occurs for at least four reasons that have been widely identified (see for example, Pahl, 1984; Renooy, 1990; Thomas, 1992; Komter, 1996; Leonard, 1998; Williams and Windebank, 1999). As indicated above (p 10), these include the barriers of lack of economic capital, lack of social network capital, lack of human capital and institutional barriers.

What might LETS do to tackle these barriers? First, they are seen to be able to address the economic capital barrier by providing people without access to national currency with interest-free credit in local currency, as well as the ability to loan tools and get work completed. Second, they are able to tackle the barrier of social network capital by providing a network of people who can be called on for help. Third, they extend human capital as LETS provide a forum in which skills can be maintained and new ones acquired, self-esteem and confidence developed (through successfully trading), and physical ability as a constraint on trading overcome due to the way that work is recognised and valued. Finally, it is thought that LETS can tackle the institutional barriers that prevent people from engaging in mutual aid by providing a formal environment which is recognised and accepted by the tax and benefit authorities.

Conclusions

This chapter has explored the rationales for extending the conceptualisation of 'bridges into work' beyond inserting people into formal jobs. Given both the problems of achieving full employment and the desire of people to rebuild a sense of community outside employment, initiatives such as LETS need to be considered, not only as a means of facilitating entry into formal employment, but also as capacity-building vehicles to develop social capital in the form of reciprocity. As such, LETS need to be evaluated in terms of their effectiveness at both improving employability and harnessing the capacity of populations to engage in mutual aid.

Taking this wider conceptualisation of work and inclusion, the effectiveness of LETS is evaluated in this report in terms of their ability to create jobs and improve employability, as well as their ability to facilitate alternative means of livelihood. To begin this task, we turn to a consideration of the first comprehensive national evaluation of LETS.

Part Two

Geographies of LETS

4

Introducing LETS

In order to evaluate whether LETS can provide a means of fuller engagement for the unemployed, we commence by examining the origins and growth of LETS in the UK. This provides the basis for an evaluation of the extent to which these schemes provide a springboard into employment, a test bed for self-employed business ventures or a bridge into reciprocal exchange networks. The research process is briefly described and the reasons for establishing LETS are examined. Finally, the current strategies for promoting LETS are discussed and activity levels considered.

The origins of LETS

The use of local currencies as bridges into work is not new. During the 1930s, 'alternative' currencies were established to combat social exclusion throughout Europe and North America (Offe and Heinze, 1992; Greco, 1994; Croall, 1997; Pacione 1997a; Boyle, 1999). For example, an experiment with local money in the Austrian town of Worgl resulted in over 300 other towns becoming interested in replicating the experience before it was terminated when the Austrian state bank threatened legal proceedings (Offe and Heinze, 1992). Learning from this experience, local currencies that have emerged since the early 1980s are viewed as 'complementary' to the national monetary system and no notes or coins are issued (Dobson, 1993; Dauncey, 1996; Seyfang, 1998). LETS are by far the most popular and widespread form of local currency system (Tibbett, 1997).

The first LETS was established in Canada in 1983 by Michael Linton, in response to the shortage of national currency in his home town of Courtenay, British Columbia. The closure of the externally-owned key industry on which the locality was heavily dependent for employment and the resulting reverse multiplier effect meant that few residents had sufficient money to buy goods and services. This prompted Linton to search for alternative ways in which they could pay. In 1985, he was invited to present a paper on his LETS idea to 'The Other Economic Summit' – a forum for 'new economics' thinkers which ran alongside the G7 Economic Summit (Linton, 1986). This workshop was the catalyst for the spread of LETS throughout the advanced economies. By 1999, there were approximately 300 LETS in France, 300 in the UK, 250 in Australia, 110 in the US, 100 in Italy, 90 in the Netherlands, 90 in Germany, 57 in New Zealand, 29 in Belgium, 27 in Canada, 19 in Austria, 1 in Switzerland, 14 in Sweden, 7 in Norway and 3 in Denmark, to name but a few of the nations to which LETS have now diffused. However, due to the lack of research on LETS in other countries, this report focuses on the nature and extent of LETS in the UK.

UK LETS schemes and LETSystems

At the outset, it is necessary to repeat that this report concentrates on what are known as LETS schemes. It does not analyse LETSystems. In the UK, nearly all LETS are based on the LETS scheme model which seeks to use local currency to foster social capital within local communities, build alternative means of livelihood and pursue ecologically sustainable development. LETSystems are yet to become widely operational in the UK and, in contrast to LETS schemes, are more 'economic' in orientation. They set out to create an alternative monetary system to the national currency by providing multiple currencies that act as an efficient and effective alternative means of exchange to formal money (see Lee et al, 2000, for further discussion of LETSystems; refer to Appendix C for a list of useful websites). Until such time as LETSystems become widely operational in the UK, however, no thorough evaluation can be made of their potential as bridges into work. Thus, this report focuses on LETS schemes.

The growth of LETS in the UK

In the UK, the first LETS was established in Norwich in 1985 (Lee, 1996). It was not until the 1990s, however, that the idea really began to take off. In early 1992, there were just five LETS in operation, 40 one year later, and 303 by 1999. Although the earlier statistics should be treated with some caution, they indicate that the growth of LETS is a late 1990s phenomenon.

A problem confronted at the start of this research was that very little information existed on even the number of LETS in the UK. The directory produced by the national coordinating agency, LETSLink UK, was quickly found to be incomplete and out of date. By contacting each of the coordinators included in this directory to find out whether their LETS existed and about other LETS known to them, we found that many either no longer functioned or had never become operational. Others were found that had not been previously identified.

In total, this process revealed that some 303 LETS were operating in the UK in 1999 (a figure inconsistent with the 400-500 often quoted in the press in recent years). Moreover, of the 37% who responded to the coordinators' survey, it was found that LETS had a mean average of 72 members and an average annual turnover equivalent to £4,668 (£64.83 per capita). Extrapolating from this, it can be estimated that there are some 21,800 LETS members in the UK who trade the equivalent of some £1.4 million worth of goods and services using local currencies.

Researching LETS

In order to provide a comprehensive evaluation of LETS as bridges into work, our research was designed in four distinct stages.

Stage 1: Survey of all UK LETS coordinators

To identify all LETS in the UK, the contacts listed in the LETSLink directory, as well as others known to the researchers, were telephoned. They were asked whether their LETS were still running and whether they knew of any other LETS in their locality. This 'snow-balling' method identified 303 LETS operational in the UK. A postal questionnaire was then sent, in 1999, to the coordinators of these schemes. A total of 113 coordinators responded (37%); of these, 72 (64%) agreed that they would participate in a membership survey.

Stage 2: Membership survey of LETS

The coordinators' survey revealed that LETS are fairly heterogeneous, half had less than 50 members and three quarters less than 90. Therefore, a stratified maximum variation sampling technique was employed to select 26 diverse LETS for a full membership survey using five key variables identified from the coordinators' survey. These were regional location, urban/rural, affluent/deprived neighbourhood, membership size and nature of pricing mechanism. Some 2,515 questionnaires were despatched to all members of these 26 contrasting LETS. Some 810 members responded (34%).

The questionnaire responses enabled analysis of the size and composition of LETS, how they operated and the ways in which they act as bridges into work for members. Both the coordinators' and membership surveys were analysed using SPSSv10.

Stage 3: Ethnographic action research

Alongside this quantitative research, two LETS in contrasting areas agreed to participate in action-orientated ethnographic research (one in semi-rural Stroud and another in the inner London borough of Brixton), enabling further exploration of both the problems and issues involved in developing LETS (see Appendix A). In each case, an initial postal questionnaire of all members was conducted followed by ethnographic action research using Stringer's (1996) 'look-think-act' methodology. This involved the researcher working with LETS coordinators and members to gain an understanding of the different meanings that members attached to their participation in LETS and the constraints on their involvement. These meanings were explored using a multitude of methods ranging from formal semi-structured interviews and focus groups through informal conversations to participation in the scheme.

Furthermore, to understand the barriers to joining LETS, groups of non-members in both localities were involved in discussions about joining LETS. This typically followed a presentation about LETS. However, because the groups involved had different ways of working and varying amounts of time available, a mixture of methods was used to access their opinions. These included questionnaires, semi-structured interviews, group discussions and question-and-answer sessions. The groups participating included job clubs, unemployment centres, ex-offender associations, parent and toddler groups, women's refuges, church groups, pensioner clubs, groups of people with physical and mental disabilities and residents' associations (for a full list of participating groups, see Appendix B).

Given the action-orientated nature of the research, the aim at the outset was that this research would be part of the development activity of both the LETS involved. Initial meetings with LETS members at members' meetings in Stroud, and Development Team meetings in Brixton, guided the research process. A number of practical outcomes resulted from this action research. For example, in Stroud, a Social Economy Forum was established. This developed into a series of meetings at which the local credit union, LETS members and time bank workers discussed methods of joint promotion via newsletters, socials and community events. In Brixton, the result was a series of community workshops where non-members met LETS members to discuss ways of extending membership and including other organisations within LETS. In addition, funding applications were completed using the data gathered and one grant for LETS training and development was successful, enabling Brixton LETS to develop its marketing.

Stage 4: Interviews with UK LETS development workers

To complete this multi-method empirical approach, in-depth face-to-face interviews were conducted with a range of LETS development workers in the UK. This enabled the research to move from an individual scheme basis to gain an understanding of the challenges facing LETS at the national and regional levels, to consider, for example, the campaign around LETS and social security benefits. In addition, specific LETS that had been strategically organised to include particular groups were involved in this process in order to explore examples of good practice from the UK.

The net outcome of this research was a survey of all 303 LETS coordinators (with a 37% response rate), 2,515 members (with a 34% response rate) and 200 non-members, coupled with 78 in-depth interviews, 13 focus groups and action-orientated ethnographic research for eight-month periods in both Stroud and Brixton LETS.

Why are LETS created?

The most common rationale for establishing a LETS was to facilitate community building (33%), followed by to combat poverty (15%), to share skills (10%), to create an alternative economy (9%), because it is a 'good idea' (8%), because the existing LETS was too far away (6%), to pursue sustainable development (4%) and to encourage local economic development (3%).

However, these rationales soon changed. Once LETS became operational, a further 29% of LETS adopted primarily community-building rather than economic rationales, such as creating an alternative economy. This was often linked to a change of personnel. Men who set up LETS had more ideological rationales (such as developing an 'alternative' to capitalism), while the reasons women founded LETS were nearly wholly grounded in practical community-building motives. Over time, men tended to drop out of their 'leadership' role (often as they became disillusioned) and women took over to pursue their more practical community-centred goals. Similar trends have been identified previously in New Zealand (Williams, 1996c) and Australia (Williams, 1997).

Promoting LETS

'Word-of-mouth' is the principal method by which knowledge of LETS is transmitted. Some 64% of LETS rely on this marketing device, not least because it is one of the few 'no cost' methods available. The employment of other methods costs sterling money that is not possessed by these 'voluntary' groups. Just 49% of all LETS had received financial (sterling) support, 75% of which came from local government. However, only 7% of all LETS had received financial support to help with publicity although these tended to have a membership profile more representative of the local community than those who had not.

Trading activity on LETS

The findings of the coordinators' survey showed that, in the LETS that responded, the average number of members was 72; the median size was between 30 and 40 and the size of membership ranged from 11 to 350. Nevertheless, the survey also illustrated that not all members were actively trading. As many as a third (33%) of members were not trading at all, and only a quarter (24%) were trading more than 10 times per annum. Low levels of trading activity were also apparent in the turnover figures, with 80% of groups reporting a turnover of less than 4,000 units for the previous year. The membership survey reinforced these findings. Only 17% of members described themselves as 'committed' to LETS, and a further 20% as regular traders, compared to the 41% who described their trading as occasional and the 20% who described themselves as supportive but not active. The reasons for these low levels of activity are explored in Chapter 11.

Conclusions

This chapter has introduced LETS by outlining how they have emerged in numbers in the UK only in the late 1990s. By 1999, the 303 operational LETS with their 21,800 members were trading the equivalent of some £1.4 million per annum in goods and services. Having outlined the multiple methods used to research these schemes and highlighted how most LETS in the UK are LETS schemes based on community-building objectives, we now turn to examining their location.

5

Mapping UK LETS

Location of LETS

The first question confronting anyone who wishes to join a LETS is whether one exists in their locality. Each LETS was asked about the size of the area that it covered. From this, an average land area covered by LETS was calculated. Extrapolating this to the 303 LETS operating in the UK, our finding is that at present, LETS cover just 16% of the UK land area (that is, 38,200 square kilometres). For the population of most areas, therefore, the main barrier to participation in LETS is that one does not exist locally. Even in the 16% of the UK where LETS existed in 1999, it cannot be assumed that all of the population are being reached. Members of rural LETS living outside the village or town in which they were based often felt marginalised from the LETS because few people contacted them either to request work or to offer to do work for them. Similarly, in cities, there was a strong sense that the LETS often belonged to, and were more used by, people living in a particular neighbourhood rather than by people in the city as a whole.

Figures 1 and 2 display the distribution of LETS and the membership of LETS in the UK. (Figure 1 is based on the identification of 303 LETS in the UK; Figure 2 draws on data supplied from the 113 LETS that returned coordinators' surveys.) The maps show that, not only has the creation of LETS tended to be concentrated in the affluent southern regions of the UK, but that the distribution of the membership is also heavily skewed towards these southern regions. In part, this skewed distribution towards the southern counties could be interpreted as a response to the greater need of lower-income population groups in the south (such as the unemployed or retired people)

for alternative means of livelihood. Higher costs of living may cause lower-income groups in southern regions to be more motivated to seek out alternative economic coping mechanisms than similar population groups living the north of the UK (see Williams, 2001). Alternatively, it could be argued that there is a close correlation between the distribution of the electorate with 'alternative' or 'green' values – which tend to be associated with predominantly affluent regions – and the geographical distribution of LETS. Whether one adopts an economic or more socio-political explanation for the geographical distribution and membership of LETS, the fact remains that they tend to be heavily clustered in relatively affluent regions of the UK.

Figure 1: Geographical distribution of LETS in the UK: by county (1999)

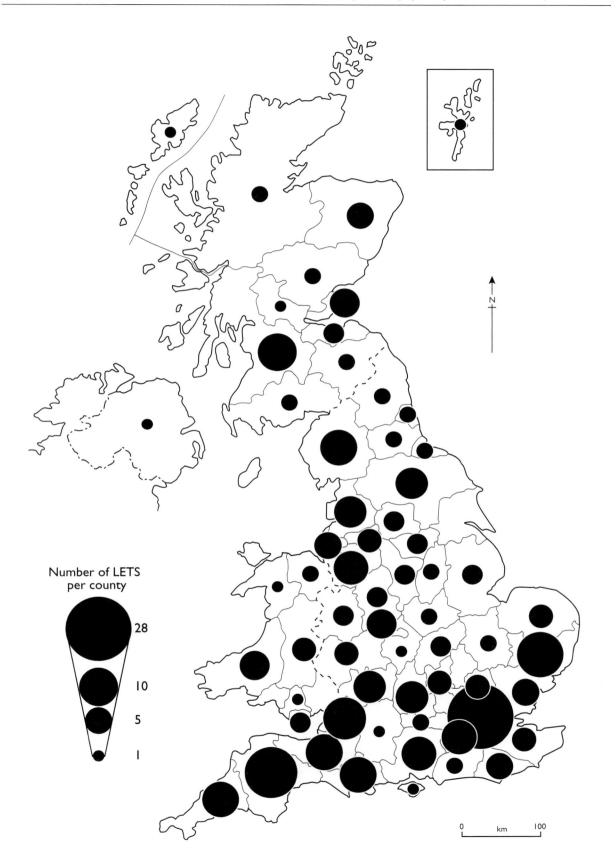

Figure 2: Geographical distribution of LETS members in the UK: by county (1999)

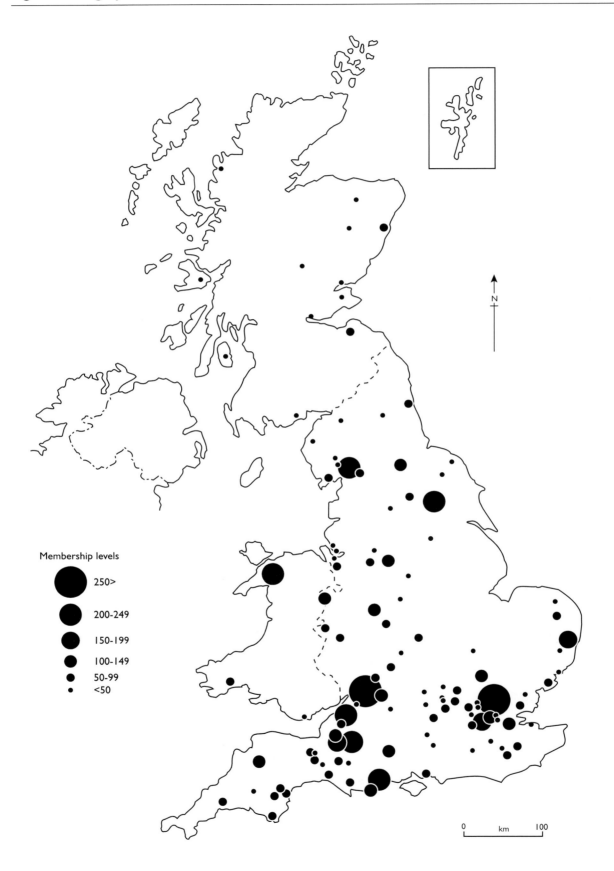

Membership levels

250>

200-249

150-199

100-149

50-99

<50

0   km   100

Conclusions

At present, LETS cover only a small proportion of the total land area of the UK. For many people, therefore, the major barrier to participation in LETS is that one does not exist in their area. However, even populations living in those areas where LETS do exist frequently feel excluded from joining and participating.

Moreover, examining the regional distribution of LETS shows that both LETS and membership of LETS tend to be heavily concentrated in affluent southern regions of the UK. In part, this might be because the higher cost of living in these areas means that low-income groups have greater need for additional coping mechanisms and, in part, it may be due to the greater concentration of 'green' or 'alternative' people in these regions.

6

LETS membership

In this chapter, we first investigate the characteristics of the membership of LETS followed by people's motivations for joining. The purpose of investigating who engages in LETS and why is to explore whether they are indeed reaching people for whom increased access to 'work' may enhance their means of livelihood.

Membership of LETS

Who joins LETS in the UK? As Table 1 shows, membership is skewed towards particular socioeconomic groups. Over two thirds of the members of these schemes are women who, in the wider society, also tend to bind community together through their reciprocal exchange activity within the extended family and social or neighbourhood networks (Williams and Windebank, 1999; Gregory and Windebank, 2000). Membership also tends to be skewed towards the 30- to 59-year-old age group and those who live in relatively low-income households (only 34% had a gross income of more than £20,000). One explanation for these low income levels could be the low percentage (19.5%) of members who are full-time employees and the high proportion who are part-time employees or self-employed. Figure 3 contrasts these percentages with the types of economic activity reported in the *Census of Population*. The figure shows that there is an under-representation of the full-time employed on LETS and an over-representation of the part-time employed, self-employed and unemployed compared with the population in general.

Table 1: Characteristics of UK LETS members (% of all survey responses)

	%
Age group	
Under 20	0.7
20-29	6.1
30-39	24.9
40-49	29.5
50-59	22.4
60-69	11.8
70 or over	4.7
Gross annual household income	
<£4,160	8.6
£4,161-6,499	7.4
£6,500-9,099	12.3
£9,100-14,299	22.7
£14,300-19,299	13.2
£19,300-24,699	11.4
£24,700-33,799	13.5
>33,800	10.9
Employment status	
Full-time employee	19.5
Part-time employee	18.4
Self-employed with employees	2.8
Self-employed without employees	25.1
Voluntary worker	1.5
Gender	
Men	31.3
Women	68.7
Disability	
Registered disabled	5.0
Registered unemployed claiming benefit	4.9
Homemaker	7.9
Student	1.4
Retired	14.6
Permanently sick	3.3
Other	0.6

Figure 3: Comparison of employment status of LETS members (1999) with the UK population (1991)

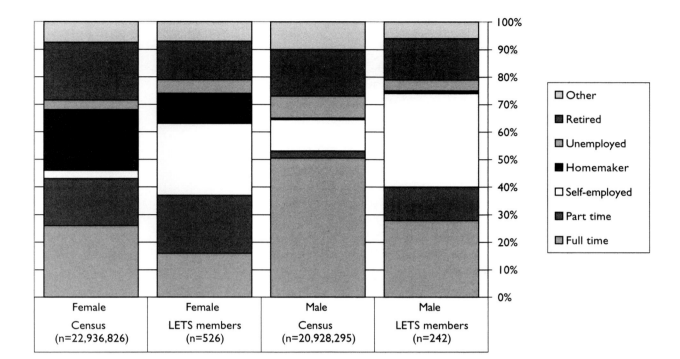

Such patterns of economic activity combined with low household incomes could be taken as surrogate indicators of social exclusion. However, when other characteristics of LETS members are considered, it indicates that a large proportion have opted out of full-time employment as a means of livelihood to take an alternative route. For example, over 60% are educated to degree level (see Table 2), suggesting they are well qualified to enter the labour market, and 48% support the Green Party (see Table 3), indicating a political orientation outside mainstream economic ideas.

Table 2: Highest educational qualifications of LETS members (% of all survey responses)

Highest qualification	%
None	2.9
Commercial	1.4
GCSE grades D-G	1.6
GCSE grades A-C (or equivalent)	7.5
A levels	4.8
Higher education (below degree)	17.9
Degree	41.9
Postgraduate	20.5
Other	1.8

Table 3: Party political orientation of LETS members (% of all survey responses)

Political party supported	%
Green	47.8
Labour	32.9
Liberal	11.8
Conservative	3.1
Other	4.4

One interpretation of LETS, therefore, is that they are principal sites for the congregation of 'down-shifters' who are disenchanted with the 'employment ethic' and want to be part of an expressive community through which they can pursue their desire to create alternatives to employment. To explore whether this is indeed the case, we here examine the reasons why people join LETS.

Why do people join LETS?

The membership survey reveals a range of motivations for joining LETS. The main reason for a quarter (25%) of members can be categorised as 'ideological'. They explicitly stated that they joined as an act of resistance to various mainstream 'others', such as capitalism, materialism, globalisation and the profit motive. For these members, LETS are 'expressive communities': acts of political protest and resistance to the 'mainstream' where ideals can be put into practice (cf, Hetherington, 1998; Urry, 2000). Such motivations suggest that, for many, joining and participating in LETS is part of an attempt to engage in creating an alternative political economy.

A further 70% explained their decision to join, not in terms of opposition to some 'other', but in more positive terms, stating that LETS provided an effective coping mechanism. For many of these participants, LETS were 'economic' vehicles for exchanging goods and services (20%), for overcoming a lack of money (12%), receiving a specific service (9%), or using particular skills (1%). For some within this group, LETS contributed towards establishing a means of livelihood that did not centre on full-time employment, while for others, albeit a minority, LETS are an important part of their route into the labour market. This latter group includes the 3% who explicitly joined to improve their employability. Interestingly, but perhaps not surprisingly, members prioritising economic motivations also tend to be those on low incomes. In contrast, the remainder of motivations can be categorised as 'social' reasons and these tend to be cited by the relatively affluent. Such social motivations include joining to meet or help others.

Conclusions

Looking at the membership and people's reasons for joining suggests that the role of LETS in people's lives can be linked to a desire to change their circumstances. This may be in terms of creating an alternative livelihood, or as a route out of economic or social marginalisation. Members tend to be non-employed and on low incomes, yet many also appear to be well qualified and to support the Green Party. In part, this reflects how LETS have marketed themselves. The use of 'word-of-mouth' as the principal marketing tool (because it costs nothing and these voluntary initiatives have little or no sterling money) means that the membership of LETS remains over-represented by those involved in the 'alternative' green movement in the UK from which the LETS movement originated. However, this should not be

over-exaggerated. Only a quarter of the members surveyed joined for mainly ideological reasons and there are now a high number of non-employed and low-income members who have joined LETS for economic reasons. In Part Three, therefore, we explore whether LETS have been able to provide them with bridges into work.

Part Three

LETS as bridges into work

7

LETS as routes into employment

A principal reason that UK government departments are currently supportive of LETS is because they are seen as a potential step towards employment for people who are unemployed (DfEE, 1999; SEU, 2000). For example, when giving Policy Action Team 1 (PAT1) its terms of reference, the Social Exclusion Unit (SEU) asked it to "consider whether participation in LETS could represent a useful transition to the open labour market" (DfEE, 1999, p 113). As PAT1 recognised, however, little hard evidence has so far been available on whether or not this is the case (DfEE, 1999). This chapter draws on the wide-ranging data collected in this study to consider three specific facets of this issue. First, we consider the number of formal jobs in this study directly created by LETS, second, their ability to act as a direct route into employment and, third, their role in indirectly acting as a pathway into employment.

No more than a handful of jobs are directly created by LETS since they are usually run by volunteers. However, some 5% of members surveyed asserted that LETS had, in a very direct way, helped them to gain formal employment. This was because working in the LETS office administering the scheme had enabled valuable skills to be acquired and used by these members to apply successfully for formal jobs. Clearly, the ability of LETS in this regard is limited as only a small number of people can play a prominent role in administering the scheme. Given that there are over 300 LETS, the scope exists for only 600-900 people to use LETS in this manner at any one time.

Nevertheless, despite the small number of people who might benefit in this way, the changes to the lives of the individuals concerned can be very important. As one 50- to 54-year-old unemployed single woman explained:

"Coming into LETS I've had a lot of interaction with other people, lots of different people, and it helps me with my confidence. I'm going to learn how to do the directory, and I've been inputting cheques into the computer accounts so I'm learning different things through my LETS work. I think I just enjoy the contact with other people and the fact that I'm getting LETS responsibilities now, it makes me feel that I'm a bit important and getting invited to meetings, it's really good. And writing up messages in the day book, someone put 'good idea, well done' – well it just makes you feel valued and that you are making a contribution.... I've been out of work for over two years and I've had problems getting references from previous employers because they say they can't remember that long ago, which is upsetting ... so I should be able to get references from the LETS for the work I'm doing, which will help in looking for paid work when I'm ready."

This is not the only way in which LETS provide a path into employment. They also improve employability more indirectly and their potential in this regard could reach a much larger number of unemployed people. LETS are able to improve employability indirectly in several ways. On the one hand, the act of participating in LETS enables skills to be maintained and new skills to be acquired. For example, many members felt that LETS were useful because they allowed skills that they possessed but which were unwanted or unvalued in the formal economy to be maintained or enhanced through their LETS exchanges. For others, LETS were a tool for acquiring new skills. Indeed, some 15% of all members asserted that LETS had enabled them to acquire new skills and this figure rose to 24% among the registered unemployed. The new skills acquired included computing, administration and interpersonal skills.

On the other hand, LETS are able to improve employability by boosting self-confidence and self-esteem. It is now well known that anything more than a very short spell of unemployment has considerable impacts on the psychological well-being of the person involved – especially in terms of their confidence and self-esteem (Engbersen et al, 1993). The result is that it becomes even more difficult for these people to reinsert themselves into the labour market. However, LETS provide a vehicle for tackling this problem of lack of confidence and self-esteem. Some 27% of all respondents asserted that LETS had boosted their self-confidence, and this was the case for 33% of the registered unemployed. Engaging in exchange on LETS was very important in this regard for a large share of the non-employed for at least two reasons. First, and given that their unemployed status meant that they often felt that their attributes were not valued by the formal economy, the act of being able to sell their services on by LETS provided them with a significant boost to their self-worth. Second, merely realising that they had something to offer was important in boosting their confidence. As one unemployed woman said:

"I sometimes go through the LETS Directory and I look at what other people offer and it's really interesting because you forget about things that you are able to do.... Sometimes I get so depressed that I think I can't do anything, and when you look through the LETS Directory and you see all these skills being offered and then you say 'Yes, I can do that too!' ...You remember all these things that you, in a way, take so much for granted that you don't even think that that is a skill, you just take it for granted and you don't use it. But if you look through the Directory and you have a lot of time on your hands and you don't kind of know what to do, then it kind of wakes you up to the fact, first of all that you're not alone ... and, secondly, it wakes you up to all the things that you can do and that's been very positive."

However, if some find that LETS provide a fillip to their confidence, it can also have the opposite effect when the services offered are not taken up by anybody. For a particular group of registered unemployed people whose services had not been purchased, participating in LETS had bruised their already fragile self-confidence even further, making them feel even worse about themselves. "If people don't even want to pay LETS for my work, then you can imagine how that makes you feel", was one such response. This group, however, constitutes only a small minority of the unemployed LETS members. It tended to be those (mostly male) unemployed who had joined for ideological reasons and who blamed the "structure of the capitalist system" for their inability to find a job who suffered when they could not sell their talents on LETS. Some 30% of those who were unemployed and had joined LETS for ideological reasons asserted that LETS had not boosted their confidence or self-esteem, and 90% of these people were men. The experience of this group, however, was far from the norm. Most of the registered unemployed either found LETS a positive, or at worst a neutral, experience.

Although not directly creating jobs or being used to any great extent to insert people directly into employment, LETS were useful in improving employability indirectly. By facilitating the maintenance and acquisition of skills as well as boosting self-confidence and self-esteem, these initiatives were providing the unemployed with greater transferable personal skills and self-confidence that would be of use to them in gaining entry into the formal labour market. In conclusion, LETS do appear to be a useful bridge into employment for a small but significant proportion of members.

It is important to note, moreover, that, if LETS are developed as bridges into employment, they will not take jobs away from the formal sector. Just 13% of the goods and services acquired on LETS would have been bought from a formal business if the LETS did not exist. Some 27% of the goods and/or services would not have been acquired without the LETS and 39% would have otherwise been acquired on a 'cash-in-hand' basis. LETS, therefore, not only create new economic activity, but are generally a means of formalising 'cash-in-hand' work rather than being a substitute for formal employment.

Policy responses

To develop LETS further as a route into employment, this report suggests that two possible policy responses could be explored. First, it endorses the current policy proposal of the SEU (2000) in its *National strategy for neighbourhood renewal: A framework for consultation*. This document proposes a pilot study to give "people new freedom to earn a little casual income or participate in a Local Exchange and Trading Scheme (LETS) without affecting their benefit entitlement" (Key idea 4). Such a proposal is a necessary, albeit insufficient (see Part Five), condition for the entry of a greater number of registered unemployed onto LETS so that they can use it as a means of gaining employment.

A second proposal that would enable LETS to provide a more direct route into employment is that LETS office workers could be funded for their administrative work under the 'voluntary' sector of New Deal. This would provide such workers with a proven means of entering the formal labour market and, at the same time, enable the more efficient running of LETS (since they would not be so reliant on volunteers for their day-to-day administration). However, it is important to be aware that such an initiative may lead to a significant reduction in the voluntary nature of LETS. Until now, most LETS have grown organically, drawing on the energy of volunteers. Such a change in the funding of workers might lead to the withdrawal of such voluntary work and to an increasing dependency of these institutions on the continuing support of the state. However, if LETS are to be used as a tool for tackling social exclusion, some form of funding will be required anyway. The volunteers that currently run LETS are not only mostly unable but also unwilling to cope with the increased workload that would result from LETS becoming more popular as ways of entering into employment. This solution is one suggestion of a potential way forward.

However, such policy responses would be strongly resisted by many LETS members who contest both the view of LETS which underlies such responses, as well as their potential impacts. Most members join LETS to forge complementary means of livelihood. Responses in focus groups and interviews revealed considerable ambivalence about increased state involvement in LETS. Thus, policies aimed to provide paid administrators would not only be seen by LETS members as failing to facilitate social inclusion, but would also be seen as diminishing the sense of collective ownership which prevails in LETS because of the voluntary nature of their operations.

Such a move to incorporate LETS into the 'workfare' state would doubtless also be heavily opposed by many others (Bowring, 1998). Before finding ways to facilitate LETS as a direct route into employment, the impacts of such policy responses on the dynamics of LETS need, therefore, to be considered.

Conclusions

In sum, although LETS do not directly *create* many jobs, they do directly help a small but significant number of people into employment, mostly by providing them with administrative training in the LETS office which is then used to gain entry to the formal labour market. However, their major contribution to improving employability is more indirect. By facilitating the maintenance and acquisition of skills as well as boosting self-confidence and self-esteem, LETS provide unemployed people with greater transferable personal skills and self-confidence that are of use to them in gaining entry into the formal labour market. Thus, LETS do appear to be a useful bridge into employment for some members. Also, as is discussed in the next chapter, the ability of LETS to create a springboard into employment is not the only way in which they facilitate insertion into the formal labour market. They are also able to act as seed-beds for nurturing people wanting to become self-employed.

LETS as facilitators of self-employment

If the role of LETS in enabling insertion into employment is indirect, the way in which these schemes act as seed-beds for the development of self-employed business ventures is not. Altogether, some 11% of LETS members asserted that their LETS had directly helped them become self-employed. There were at least three ways in which LETS acted as effective incubators of new self-employed enterprises.

First, the LETS had enabled them to develop their client base (cited by 41% of those who were self-employed). As a man aged 35-39 seeking to become self-employed stated during a focus group discussion:

"I was looking to start off as a freelance journalist, at the time, and it [joining LETS] was just another way of generating some work and some contacts and building up experience without having to put in, sort of, the risk of hard currency."

Second, LETS are able to ease the cash flow of new self-employed businesses. This was cited as an important factor by 29% of those who were self-employed. An illustration of how LETS works in this way was given by a single parent on Income Support, who was setting set herself up as a self-employed massage therapist and had transferred to Family Credit. She explained:

"I became a LETS member and used the LETS as a source to advertise my services, and from this I have managed to go self-employed. All of my customers are coming through the LETS and my business is slowly building up. The LETS has been extremely important in this development both financially and the community support it provides – I get my childcare paid for through the LETS which enables my business development. LETS

has enabled my survival. At the moment life is very tight, I'd be desperate without LETS."

Third, LETS enable the development of self-employed business ventures by providing a test bed for products and services. Indeed, nearly all those who defined themselves as self-employed attributed this role to LETS. One stated:

"We joined as a way of getting into doing things on quite a small scale without having to have this big risk thing of going into it as a small business. So I make things – arts and crafts stuff – which I can sell through the LETS and sort of get an idea of what people actually like. I found it really useful as a way of getting back into making things again, and it really does boost your confidence being able to sell your stuff. If I'm selling it for money, a lot of people don't have that much excess money to spend on stuff, but they've got a lot of excess LETS, so, yeah, they can buy your things. It's like 'ooh, someone wants to buy my stuff, it must actually be alright', so you sort of go back and make more knowing that it is actually okay."

An analysis of the data from the membership survey provides some indication of the types of self-employed businesses that members are trying to develop. It shows that the most recent income generated by self-employed members on LETS was through health and personal services (31%). Those who last traded health and personal services specified their professions in some of the following ways: chiropractor, acupuncturist, shiatsu masseuse, nutritionist, aromatherapist, herbalist, reiki therapist, osteopath, reflexologist, yoga teacher and Alexander technique therapist. The most recent sales of other self-employed members included business services (8%), gardening and horticulture (7%), educational services (6%), household goods (6%), food and produce (6%), arts/crafts (5%), building and house maintenance (5%), music and entertainment (5%) and household services (4%).

This reveals three key issues about the nature of the self-employed business enterprises being developed through LETS:

1. They are mostly involved in the provision of personal services.
2. They are selling the 'alternative'.
3. Finally, they are attempting to develop self-employed ventures that formalise and legitimate their interests in providing coping mechanisms for others.

Conclusions

LETS appear to be useful seed-beds for developing self-employed business ventures (even if the businesses being developed fall within a quite narrow range of activity). In order further to facilitate this role of LETS, one possible policy response is to encourage those currently operating as self-employed in LETS to enter the 'self-employment' option in New Deal and to recognise their trading on LETS as part of their attempt to become self-employed. Indeed, other people setting out on the 'self-employment' option under New Deal could be encouraged to join their local LETS as a way to develop their client base, ease any cash flow difficulties and develop a test bed for their products and/or services. Again, however, such policy proposals would be strongly resisted by many LETS members who contest both the instrumentalist view of LETS underlying such responses as well as their potential impacts. As highlighted in Chapter 7, responses in focus groups and interviews revealed considerable ambivalence towards increased state involvement in LETS. Policies aimed at using LETS to facilitate self-employment would be seen by LETS members as failing further to facilitate the promotion of a broader notion of social inclusion and a wider view of work.

9

LETS as vehicles for mutual aid

We have shown so far that LETS act as routes into the formal labour market by both improving employability and providing a seed-bed for the development of self-employed business ventures. But these are not the only ways that LETS act as bridges into work. Adopting a wider conceptualisation of work and inclusion, LETS also provide members with access to reciprocal exchange networks. Indeed, many members saw this dimension as being the principal value of LETS. To explore the contribution of LETS to facilitating reciprocal exchange, we here assess how they are able to tackle the barriers to participation in reciprocity identified earlier (see Chapter 3).

However, before doing so, it is important to outline the history of the development of mutual aid. Historically, there have been two dominant approaches whose origins lie in the work of Smiles (1866) and Kropotkin (1902):

- the laissez-faire approach sees mutual aid as a *substitute* for employment and the welfare state; there is an appeal to duties and mutuality is perceived in terms of individuals engaged in a form of self-help;
- the 'assisted' mutual aid approach that seeks to *supplement*, rather than substitute, employment and state provision. It emphasises discretion and choice rather than the conservative appeal to duties, and envisages mutual aid as collective and interactive rather than as isolated, compliant and competitive (Evers and Wintersberger, 1988).

Most people involved in developing LETS as a vehicle for mutual aid are firmly grounded in the latter approach. Reflecting ideas in 'green economics'

(Dobson, 1993; Lang, 1994; Douthwaite, 1996; Barry and Proops, 2000), these people view LETS as a means of bringing about self-reliant sustainable communities. Support for LETS as a means of assisting mutual aid, however, is not confined to green economics. There is also a radical social democratic tradition supportive of LETS. This views the future of work and welfare in a mixed economy where civil society is a third sector that complements private and public sector provision (Giddens, 1998; Gorz, 1999; Beck, 2000). Indeed, it is for this reason that New Labour has shown such an interest in LETS in particular, and rebuilding social capital more generally (cf Putnam, 2000).

The key question for these activists and analysts, therefore, is whether LETS are able to tackle the barriers to participation in mutual aid that were identified in Chapter 3. Can they tackle the thin social networks of the unemployed? Are they able to overcome the economic constraints that prevent participation in mutual aid? Do they enhance the human capital of participants? And are they a way of addressing the institutional barriers that hinder engagement in reciprocal exchange?

In this chapter we present some evidence in response to these questions, which suggests that LETS have a positive role to play in overcoming barriers to the development of mutuality. However, these findings must be set against those presented in Chapter 10 which explores the barriers to joining and participation in LETS and, hence, to the possibilities for a wider group of people to experience and engage in enhanced practices of mutual aid.

The problem of social network capital

One of the principal reasons that many people do not engage in reciprocal exchange is because, quite simply, they either do not know anybody to call on for help or to offer help to, or they do not know people well enough to ask them to do something or to receive help (Renooy, 1990; Komter, 1996; Williams and Windebank, 2000; Williams et al, 2001).

This study reveals that LETS help tackle this issue by providing access to social networks. In Chapter 4 we indicated that an important reason people join LETS is to meet others in order to create a greater sense of community and help each other out. Reasons for this could be linked to the fact that many members are unemployed. It is now well known that this group tends to have relatively thin social networks, meaning that they have few people on whom they can call for help (see Williams and Windebank, 2001a). Another reason could be the lack of local kinship networks among many members. Some 95.3% of LETS members had no grandparents living in the area, 79.5% no parents, 84.3% no brothers or sisters, 58.2% no children, 92.6% no uncles or aunts and 90.8% no cousins. The absence of kin in the locality means that many LETS members are unable to draw on kinship exchange, the principal source of social support in contemporary society (Williams and Windebank, 2001a).

The membership survey results throw further light on how LETS are effective in expanding the breadth and depth of social support structures. Some 75% of respondents (82% of the registered unemployed) asserted that LETS had helped them to develop a network of people on whom they could call for help, 55% that it had helped them develop a wider network of friends (68% of the registered unemployed) and 30% deeper friendships. Consequently, the vast majority of members view LETS as effective for developing 'bridging' social network capital (that is, bringing people together who did not previously know each other – what Granovetter (1973) calls 'the strength of weak ties'. Slightly fewer, but still over a half of all members, also view LETS as effective in developing 'bonding' social network capital (that is, bringing people who already know each other closer together). As such, LETS appear to be effective mechanisms for developing social network capital, an issue that has received increasing attention in recent years (see for example, Home Office, 1999; Putnam, 2000).

The important role that LETS can play in developing social networks was brought out in numerous interviews and focus group discussions. Often, the people who benefited from this role of LETS were those who had recently moved to the area. Take, for example, the following extracts from a focus group discussion:

Discussant 1:   "We joined LETS only a year ago, but moving to a new area you don't have your family and friends readily laid on, and it's a very good way to get to know people.... If you haven't got anybody, or you don't know your neighbours very well, then it's a great way of asking people to do something a bit silly that you wouldn't be able to do. The first person we contacted, we wanted something moving and we couldn't lift it ourselves and we thought, 'oh, we've got no neighbours', or 'they're old neighbours', so it was sort of the introduction to LETS." (part-time employed woman, aged 30-34)

Discussant 2:   "We didn't actually know anyone to help us carry something." (full-time employed woman, aged 30-34)

Discussant 1:   "So it was as simple as that, so that was the starting point and now we're just looking to get into debt and spend more LETS and get involved that way."

Another example of the importance of LETS in developing social networks was highlighted in the following interview extract with an unemployed person:

"When I first moved here, I was finding it very, very hard to meet people, make friends. People are very reserved around this area, they don't sort of welcome strangers with open arms; so I thought I could meet people through the LETS system, and that's worked really well.... You see that's the one thing about being on benefits, low-income, it's exceedingly useful [LETS], it's a way of, instead of barely existing, you know, it enables you to do a lot of things, and its good. And, like, I was very isolated when I first moved here and through the LETS I don't feel so isolated at all

now; I've got lots of people I know to speak to, and I've got a couple of very good friends. It's great – there's a network of people available."

Economic capital

A further barrier to engaging in reciprocal exchange is a lack of money and access to the necessary equipment. LETS can provide people with a means of exchange not otherwise available to them. Some 40% of members asserted that LETS had provided them with access to interest-free credit (62% of the registered unemployed and 51% of low-income households) and some 84% stated that LETS had helped them engage in meaningful and productive activity. For two thirds (65%) of the registered unemployed, this activity had helped them cope with unemployment, with some 3% of their total income coming from their LETS activity, as well as a strong sense that they were contributing to their community. On the one hand, therefore, the role of LETS in providing access to reciprocal exchange networks was important because it enabled members to engage in productive and meaningful activity for the good of the community. On the other hand, it was important because it provided access to sources of support so that members could get necessary work completed.

Tackling the barrier of human capital

Besides tackling the barriers of economic and social network capital, there is also evidence that LETS tackle the barriers of human capital that can constrain participation in reciprocity. As discussed above, LETS provide an opportunity both to maintain and develop skills, as well as to rebuild self-confidence and self-esteem by engaging in activity that is valued and recognised by others. However, interviews with non-members reveal that some people are not able to overcome this barrier (see Chapter 11 for a detailed analysis of this problem).

Tackling institutional barriers

Finally, there is an institutional barrier to participating in reciprocal exchange. Many who are unemployed are fearful of being reported to the authorities, even if they engage only in unpaid mutual aid (see Williams and Windebank, 2001b). This is not currently being overcome by LETS. Although only 13% of members are worried about tax liabilities and 12% about reductions in welfare payments, 65% of registered unemployed members are concerned that their participation in LETS might result in their benefits being reduced. This would occur if their activity on LETS was treated as earnings and they were considered to have received sums over the 'earnings disregard'. This fear is also true of non-members. All non-members interviewed who were registered unemployed expressed grave concerns that their trades would result in a reduction in benefits and this makes them wary of joining LETS. Ironically, therefore, those who would most benefit from LETS are discouraged from joining and trading because of the uncertainty over their legal position vis-à-vis the earnings disregard. The current laissez-faire approach of government towards the regulation of LETS is therefore insufficient to appease people who are registered unemployed.

Conclusions

The previous two chapters have shown that, for those who join LETS, the schemes enable improvements in their employability and provide an incubator for developing self-employed business ventures. In this chapter, we have also revealed that LETS are bridges into work in a wider sense. Adopting a broader view of inclusion and 'work', LETS have here been shown to help create livelihoods beyond employment. By helping people to overcome many of the barriers that prevent participation in mutual aid, LETS represent complementary social inclusion policies that facilitate engagement in reciprocal exchange and develop social capital. Indeed, it is in this role that LETS are perhaps most effective at promoting fuller engagement.

Given that LETS appear to be relatively effective – not only as routes into employment and facilitators of self-employment, but also as vehicles for mutual aid – the question that needs to be answered is why so few people, especially the registered unemployed, have joined them, and why the level of activity on LETS is so low.

Part Four

Barriers to participation in LETS

10

Barriers to joining LETS

Why do so few people join LETS? In this chapter we summarise the findings of our research with groups of non-members, to examine in detail the specific barriers to joining LETS. Research of this nature has not been reported before despite its importance. Here, we provide an in-depth examination that identifies the key questions that people ask when they consider joining LETS. If LETS are to move beyond their rather narrow membership bases to become more inclusive, then the barriers to joining for these wider groups will need to be more fully considered. First, therefore, we document the research method used to investigate the barriers to joining LETS for non-members and, following this, we explore the 'weighing-up' process that people tend to go through when considering whether or not to join.

In order to explore why people do or do not join LETS, identifiable groups of non-members in Stroud and Brixton were contacted to see if it would be possible for a researcher to attend a group meeting and discuss LETS with the people present. Specific groups were targeted for inclusion in this research process. Both older and younger people, people with disabilities (including people with mental health problems), black and ethnic minority groups, unemployed non-graduates and single parents were approached. Given the diversity of these groups, the research approach was necessarily flexible with a mixture of approaches being used, including surveys, interviews and discussion groups, as well as question-and-answer sessions.

In total, 19 groups participated in this research (see Appendix B for a list of the groups involved), through which 200 people were consulted about joining LETS. By targeting groups of people who experience various forms of social exclusion and involving them in this process, we believe that this research makes some headway towards understanding the current under-representation of these groups on LETS.

Who had heard of LETS?

In order to assess the level of awareness, all participants were asked whether they had heard of LETS. In Brixton only 7% of those questioned had heard of LETS. In Stroud the percentage of people who had heard of LETS rose to 49%. This difference probably reflects the greater visibility of LETS in Stroud compared to Brixton. In Stroud, the LETS had attracted regular local media coverage and a number of local shops on the high street had, at various times, accepted payment in local currency for items purchased, thus increasing its prominence locally. Awareness of the scheme was thus far greater in Stroud than in Brixton. However, even in Stroud, where non-members had heard of the scheme, knowledge was only partial. Thus, a key barrier to joining LETS is awareness of their existence and knowledge of how they operate. This overall lack of awareness indicates that there remains a great deal of work to do in promoting their existence and marketing these schemes to different groups. It also suggests that place is an important determinant of knowledge and awareness. If LETS become a 'normal' part of local life, their practical significance enhances their visibility and, so, awareness and acceptability are increased.

How do people decide whether or not to join LETS?

Once participants had been informed of their existence, it appeared that a 'weighing-up' process took place whereby people asked five key questions when considering whether or not to join:

- Is it credible?
- Is it for me?
- What will I get out of it?
- What are the costs of involvement?
- What have I got to offer?

Table 4 summarises this weighing-up process that non-members went through when considering joining LETS and the types of queries that non-members raised at each stage of this process. In the following description, each of these questions is explored in detail.

Table 4: Barriers to joining LETS: weighing-up processes

Weighing-up process	Issues raised by non-members
Is it credible?	Usefulness of local currency Debt as positive Lack of regulation Individual pricing of goods and services
Is it for me?	Cultural identity of the organisation and who it included (location of socials, the types of businesses on LETS, exclusivity of promotional material)
What will I get out of it?	Immediate needs not met through LETS The quality of goods and services on offer
What are the costs of involvement?	Costs of joining, time, transport Lack of clarity about how benefits are affected by LETS earnings
What have I got to offer?	Skill identification How to transfer formal skills to informal economy

Is it credible?

One of the primary issues for non-members when deciding whether or not to join was their assessment of its credibility. For most non-members, credibility was entwined with issues surrounding the usefulness of a local currency, the idea that debt was something positive, the lack of regulation and the idea that it was up to the people involved to price their goods and services.

Some non-members were cautious about the idea of a local currency because they did not see it as a workable or credible alternative. A typical reaction was: 'Are people really committed to it?'. Others supported the idea, but immediately questioned its usefulness. A discussion between two Stroud men is indicative:

"Right, well I think it's a good idea – it's like tit for tat. But I'd need a lot more information on it, and you need a lot of people in it or you'll end up with a lot of Strouds and nothing to spend them on."

"I'm on JSA [Jobseekers' Allowance]. If I could go to shops and spend them then it would help. No, I don't think it's for me. It just seems too patchy."

Moreover, some non-members did not like the idea of using cheques and sought a universal means of exchange rather than a unit of account:

"See if I've got 10 LETS they're no use to me if they're stuck in a cheque book. I want to be able to say that I've got 10 LETS in my pocket and that I can go out and spend them, you know go for a night out on them. I want them as a currency, I don't want a cheque book. No, I want them as a currency, like notes, that I can count into my pocket and know that I can spend them. Make it a new currency, and you feel like you've got something."

People also found it difficult to conceive of a system that positively encouraged 'debt'. This was particularly an issue for older people who had spent their lives trying to avoid debt. Even when the notion of being 'in commitment' was explained, people still thought of debt as an overdraft. As one explained:

"Why would I want to create another overdraft, when I've got enough problems managing my other debts?"

The idea that debt is positive added to confusion around the operation of LETS. It is another layer of complexity making the idea less accessible to particular groups.

Many non-members expressed concerns about the lack of regulation on LETS. Overall, there was a widespread lack of trust with regard to using people that they did not know. For example, many of the women interviewed identified a need for childcare but said that they would not trust anyone outside the family to look after their children. One woman stated:

"I've only had babysitters when I've known the person very well. I wouldn't just 'phone them up from the directory. No, I couldn't use it like that."

Others, particularly pensioners and people with disabilities, said that they would feel vulnerable letting people they did not know into their homes. This kind of distrust reflected a more general concern that many LETS do not require police checks, references of work and details about qualifications before allowing people to join. Again, this raises issues about formalisation and state involvement that would be resisted by many members.

Some non-members thought that the notion that it was up to the people involved to determine the price also presented difficulties. They did not agree with individuals setting prices for their work:

"How do you know what to charge? You'd get your accountants wanting more than your gardeners wouldn't you – how would you earn enough? I'd want everyone to be equal, everyone should get paid the same."

Similarly, another man said:

"It's got to be fair as well, you've got to make it so that everyone gets the same rate, you've got to go into it on equal grounds. Say we all work for five LETS an hour, then you're on equal terms and no one's up there, and no one's down there. You've got to have a basis, it's like starting over a whole new world and you need to get your customers."

These responses raise fundamental questions both about value and about the value of LETS. The conflict between expectations derived from

understandings of, and practices in, the 'formal' economy and those within the 'informal' is clearly apparent.

Is it for me?

Many non-members perceived LETS as something for other people. In Stroud, people commented that "it seems like a very Stroud thing". When questioned further about this they highlighted Stroud's "wacky alternative image", and said that, "this would be exactly where LETS would take off". However, non-members also felt that the cultural identity of the scheme excluded some people. For instance, one described how the office projected a certain image:

"See I wouldn't go down there, where the office is, it's all drop-outs down there, everyone here thinks like that, it needs a better image."

Others argued that the shops accepting local currency were those they did not use. In addition, because socials were held in a particular café, the identity of LETS as something for "middle-class greenies" was further entrenched.

In Brixton non-members also raised similar issues:

"My impression of it from this directory is that it's very middle class, full of professional people."

But, in contrast to Stroud, race was also an issue. Non-members often described LETS as 'not for me':

"I don't feel like I'm represented in the literature you've shown me. It doesn't seem to be promoting awareness of black and ethnic minority involvement in LETS, simply by the lack of 'colour' in these promotional materials."

What will I get out it?

One reason some people require more convincing about the credibility of LETS is because they actually *need* LETS to work. As one non-member expressed it:

"I don't want to, well, I can't risk getting involved in another situation that isn't going to work."

Their hesitation is often because goods that could meet their most immediate material needs are not available on LETS. As a Brixton man stated:

"At the top of my shopping list is food and a few clothes, so you need a shop on it that sells cheap food ... that would give more people the motivation to participate."

Another non-member stated:

"If there's no money in it, why would I want to join it? I'm working the hardest I can to get money to pay for all the things the kids need. I'm doing the course here, and then I'm cabbying three nights a week, I'm exhausted. I couldn't give any energy to it unless it's money so I can get nappies for my girl."

This extract also highlights how many people do not have the energy to devote to something that is unlikely to meet their immediate needs.

In addition, there was a concern that the goods and services on offer might be 'second rate': "So, you're paying in this Monopoly money, is it substandard stuff then?". This question again exposes the evaluative links between the LETS economy and the mainstream. It points to a desire to be included in mainstream economic activities rather than 'making do' with what appears to be second-rate commodities in a second-class economy.

Potential demand is further dampened because some non-members did not need LETS because they already had strong social support networks and felt no need to create additional networks of support. One non-member stated, "I do favours with friends and family, I wouldn't trust anyone else to come into the home". Another identified that they already operate within existing informal money-lending systems that exist outside LETS:

"No, you see I wouldn't need a system to get interest-free credit. We all lend each other money all the time, its £50 here and there, small loans to get things sorted quickly and there's no interest."

For those already possessing either strong or dense social networks, LETS are of only marginal significance. Instead, they are most useful to those lacking such informal support infrastructures but who wish to develop their social network capital.

What are the costs of involvement?

If a potential member feels it credible, something for them and believes that there is something to be gained by joining, a further stumbling block is the cost of joining and participating (be it in terms of money, time and so on). A number of non-members reported that they found the notion of paying a joining fee a barrier, especially as there were no guaranteed returns. As one man suggested:

"Why should we have to pay to join? I don't pay to join a bank do I? You should be paying us to join. Look, people are frightened of something new, I haven't got £7 to fork out on something that's a gamble. I don't know its going to work for me. How much am I going to be able to use it? Why don't you give them 10 LETS credits or even a 100 when they join, then you've got them hooked, you've got to give some incentive to join."

Another issue among non-members was the cost in terms of time. Again it was not necessarily the idea of LETS that people were opposed to but what they felt they could give to LETS for uncertain returns. As a Brixton woman stated:

"It's a good idea, but it's not something that I'd use. I don't get a lot of time, what with the children. I really don't have time with the children."

Childcare responsibilities were a frequent reason why many women felt that they could not participate in LETS. But many other non-members also felt that a lack of time was an issue. This was because they had many other commitments such as voluntary work or caring for relatives.

Another cost for many participants was the potential travel that would be involved. This was a particular issue for people with disabilities. As one said, "Transport is my major problem: how would I get to do different trades?". It is not only the availability, but also the cost of transport, that was an issue:

"I'd have to probably travel to do the trade, so it would cost me to do the job, and then I'd get Monopoly money. No, it's not for me."

This issue of involvement costs is exacerbated by people's fears about their state benefit being affected.

"If I did join, I'd have to tell them [DSS] wouldn't I? It's a bit difficult, it would have to be thought about."

For many, therefore, the costs of joining in terms of money, time or the potential risks involved turned them away from joining LETS.

What have I got to offer?

A final barrier to joining for non-members was not knowing if they could do anything on LETS to earn some local money. Some did not perceive themselves as having any skills to offer that people might pay for:

"It sounds quite interesting. I don't know what I'd offer though – that's why I'm here at the Job Club."

"I haven't really got transferable skills. Do you think people need heavy engineering in the home?"

It is likely that these members do have skills to offer but as Barnes et al (1996) suggest, people who have not been employed for some time – particularly men – find it difficult to consider skills away from the formal labour market. Instead, they believe that if they have no skills that the formal labour desires, they have no skills at all that people might desire.

Conclusions

This chapter has shown that the first reason many do not join LETS is quite simply that they have never heard about them. Once people know about them, there is a weighing-up process that takes place. This involves people balancing the resources that they would have to commit (including time and energy) with the rewards that they might receive from joining. Many expressed that, on balance, joining was too much of a risk. Therefore, for LETS to be used by a wider cross-section of society, the factors that lead them to this conclusion will need to be altered. This will involve:

- making LETS appear more credible by displaying to non-members that LETS are 'something for them';
- showing clearly that they will get something out of joining;
- reducing the costs of involvement;

- persuading people that they have something to offer (as those who join LETS quickly discover).

How this might be achieved is addressed in Chapter 12. However, we first consider the barriers to increased trading on LETS in Chapter 11.

Barriers to increased trading on LETS

Introduction

Having identified the barriers to joining LETS, this chapter explores the barriers to increased trading confronted by people once they have taken the decision to join. One of the key findings of this study, as identified in Chapter 4, was the low level of trading on LETS. The reasons given by current LETS members for the overall low levels of activity are examined in order to understand what prevents existing members from using LETS more fully as routes into work. Although low levels of trading have been a constant theme in LETS literature (see Aldridge and Patterson, 2001), it has often been explained in terms of LETS being in their infancy and the belief that trading should increase as LETS move beyond their start-up phase and mature. However, after 10 years of UK LETS development, we question the validity of this explanation. It seems vital that, if LETS are to be effective bridges into work for the unemployed and others, there must be a more critical examination of why low trading levels persist. This analysis first draws on data from the national survey to provide a general introduction to barriers to increased trading in LETS, then goes on to consider data collected through action research within Stroud and Brixton LETS. This data draws on interview material, focus groups, SWOT analysis, community workshops and active participation in LETS.

The impacts of low trading levels on LETS are serious. Not only does the narrow range of goods and services that appear to be on offer discourage people from joining, but low trading also leads to the withdrawal of members and, in some cases, the closure of LETS. For example, during the course of our research, 26 LETS were identified that had closed down through lack of use, while a further four LETS were described as 'dormant', in that trading had temporarily ceased pending an upsurge in interest.

Furthermore, within individual LETS, a typical pattern is that there are a core of active traders (25% of members), a segment of occasional traders (50%) and an outer periphery of non-traders (25%). Thus, while the current estimate of the UK LETS population is 21,800 (see Chapter 4), there is an active population of only some 5-6,000 members. Nevertheless, it must be understood that for some LETS members, it is the act of joining and identification with the various aims of this organisation that is as important as the trading. For example, as a Stroud member put it:

"For me, I've always been interested in things to do with creating possibilities, in particular, new economic possibilities, and alternative ways that human beings can interact with each other to introduce elements of freedom. So for me, joining LETS is important because it represents the importance of being part of social processes around constructing alternatives."

It is important not to deny LETS members' philosophical and ideological reasons for joining LETS (Barry and Proops, 2000; Lee et al, 2000). However, it is also necessary to understand the barriers to increased trading and to make recommendations for the future direction of LETS so that those who wish to develop them can be helped to do so.

In the membership survey, LETS members were asked to identify what they considered to be the main barriers to regular trading in LETS. The principal barriers included:

- a lack of time to engage in LETS trading (71% of respondents);
- the non-availability of goods and services through LETS (49%);
- need for sterling (47%);
- anxiety about tax/benefits (13%).

These barriers were explored in detail with LETS members in Stroud and Brixton, where, despite the contrasting case study locations, the barriers to LETS development were very similar. Table 5 provides a summary. Three principal barriers to increased trading in LETS were identified:

1. organisational capacity;
2. negotiating trades
3. the size of LETS.

Here, we explore each barrier in turn. It should be noted that, in this chapter, we confine ourselves to the changes required in the internal operating environment of LETS. The changes necessary in the external operating environment of LETS are considered in Chapter 12.

Table 5: Barriers to increased trading in LETS

Type of barrier	LETS members identified
Organisational capacity	Shortage of people willing/able to get involved
	Out-of-date information
	Lack of visibility
	Developmental resources
Negotiating trades	Skill identification and pricing work
	Qualifications and quality
Size of LETS	Access to goods and services
	Circulation of goods and services

The barrier of organisational capacity

LETS require a certain amount of organisation and administration to function effectively. In many instances, a core group consisting of between 4 and 10 members conducts the tasks that need to be carried out. While this core group is often made up of people committed to LETS, problems do arise.

Shortage of people willing/able to get involved

In both Stroud and Brixton LETS, there was seen to be a shortage of people willing or able to take part in the organisation of the LETS. In Brixton the development team regularly went through "peaks and troughs":

"We'll go through six months where people are really committed and we make lots of decisions and progress, only to be – six months later – back where we started with the accounts not updated, or half of the accounts on one person's computer and another half on another system that isn't working. It takes an awful lot of energy and tolerance to stay with it for an extended period because you feel like you're really treading water."

One of the main issues is that members of the core group often experience 'burnout':

"It [LETS administration] *can be a thankless task; I often think why I am doing this? And I'm spending hours and hours a week doing it."*

"Sometimes people think we are a bank, you know, it's done voluntarily and it's a lot of work."

Burnout often occurs because numbers dwindle and then core group tasks have to be picked up by the fewer remaining core group members. It is also exacerbated by a lack of resources – particularly the absence of an accessible shared space for LETS work as well as limited and outdated equipment.

Out-of-date information

The shortage of people willing to organise schemes means that the information required for LETS to run effectively – notably the directory of goods and services wanted and provided – frequently becomes out of date. This presents difficulties when members attempt to arrange trading:

"When I rang around, probably half of those were no longer living at the place where they were or didn't want

to be involved, and so there weren't that many people that seemed really active on the scheme."

For occasional traders, when they did try to access goods or services, many telephone calls would have to be made, which would not necessarily result in a trade being organised. This meant that members failed to see results from their involvement, which led to dissatisfaction with LETS as a viable form of trading. For active traders, the lack of efficiency in accounting and administration caused much frustration and resulted in a reluctance to trade. As a Brixton LETS member pointed out:

"The 'massage crew', as we call them, have been really frustrated because cheques have gone missing and their accounts haven't been updated for the work they've done. We've got really detailed letters of the work they have done and they want to know where the accounts are. And it's understandable because they have done a lot of work through the scheme."

This issue is further exacerbated in urban areas where people tend to move more frequently:

"We have this tremendous turnover of population. I mean the Electoral Roll for example has a 30% turnover a year, so it is a problem. But there is a core community that doesn't move very much and I suppose it's tapping into that."

Moreover, members often forget to inform the LETS when they move home.

Another reason why directories include people who are no longer trading is because some LETS are reluctant to lose members. This is because schemes recognise the problems of being small scale and want to hold onto as many members as possible in the hope that they might resume trading. Thus, there is an issue of the trade-off between creating 'leaner', more dynamic LETS, composed of trading members, and maintaining larger, less efficient schemes, that appear to have more to offer potential joiners.

Lack of visibility

Neither the Brixton scheme nor even the Stroud scheme was very visible in the local community although the Stroud scheme was more so. This meant

that people wanting to join LETS often found it difficult to get information about them. One said:

"It doesn't publicise itself at all. It took me ages to join – I ended up finding the address in the library, but before then I'd tried for quite a few months to actually track it down. And the local council knew nothing about it, the library knew nothing about it or these sort of local community information places – they hadn't heard of it or weren't able to push me in the right sort of direction. So it's got a low profile within Lambeth."

This delay often had repercussions for trading. As another member stated:

"This really doesn't help to get you trading; the momentum was lost."

Lack of visibility was more of an issue in Brixton because it is a geographically complex urban environment. The Stroud scheme, meanwhile, with its high-street presence in this 'alternative' milieu is slightly more visible.

Despite these problems, some members have concerns about making LETS more visible. They felt that if they promoted the scheme too widely they might attract "the wrong type of people", by which they meant people who would spend but not earn local currency or people who would abuse the trust required for LETS to function. These members either actively try to prevent any broadening of the membership base or are reticent about LETS development strategies. Joining LETS as an act of resistance to some mainstream 'others' such as capitalism, materialism, globalisation and the profit motive, they view LETS as a site where like-minded people can congregate and engage in acts of political protest and resistance to the 'mainstream'. Any widening of the membership base would 'water down' the 'alternative' nature of LETS.

Developmental resources

To administer LETS is not a quick and easy task. It requires a great deal of time and effort. Both the LETS studied in depth found it difficult to find time to discuss how to increase trading. As one member of the Stroud office team stated:

"We're not talking about developing the scheme. All we discuss is renewal dates, who's doing the newsletter, and when shall we have the next 'trading day'. We're not looking at how this scheme is going to develop. And that's because it's more work on top, and we haven't got the people to do it. So the LETS is just sustaining itself within the niche of people you'd expect to be in it. It feels a bit stuck."

In Stroud, therefore, although the LETS administration systems are in place, it is difficult to move beyond this because all of their resources are taken up in managing these processes. Ideas did not constrain LETS development in Brixton but progress could not be made until the administrative systems were in place:

"We've got loads of ideas about how to develop this scheme, but without the people to do the administration – which can be boring – we can't progress, because we haven't got the necessary procedures in place for simply ensuring accounts will be produced and newsletters distributed."

These quotes indicate the tensions that many groups experience in the trade-off between administration and the development of LETS.

The barrier of negotiating trades

Besides the organisational barriers that prevent increased trading on LETS, there are also barriers related to the negotiation of trades. Here we consider the two principal forms that these barriers take.

Skill identification and pricing work

Some new members encountered problems when beginning to trade. Often this was because of a lack of confidence in the skills that they had to offer and the prices to charge for them (see Aldridge et al, 2001: forthcoming). To overcome such difficulties, both schemes encouraged new members to get involved with the LETS administration. For a number of LETS members this was their introduction to LETS trading. In both LETS, 'office workers' (Stroud) and members of the 'development team' (Brixton) were paid a standard rate for administration. This was found by many new

members to resolve their difficulties with pricing. As a Brixton LETS member puts it:

"People involved in administering the LETS charge a standard price for this work, so I now use the standard because it avoids having to think about pricing and makes the whole thing a lot easier."

Qualifications and quality

Another set of barriers included members feeling unable to ask others for details of their qualifications and this left them anxious about the quality of goods or services. As one stated:

"I'd find it quite hard to say, 'What are your qualifications for doing this job?' because I think there's a feeling that you might be undermining that person, but then it's a completely legitimate thing to ask them.... There's a kind of feeling that because it's not real money that you don't have that power and place to do that, which is just ridiculous and I know people would say, 'Well it's your right to do that', but I did feel that was a problem for me."

In Stroud, LETS members were encouraged to indicate the level of skills they had. Details were noted in the directory where appropriate and LETS members were also encouraged to provide recommendations of good work accessed through LETS, which were written up in the newsletter. These strategies helped to provide more information about traders and lessened anxiety around LETS trading.

Size of LETS

The final set of barriers to participation in trading on LETS revolved around the size of LETS. These barriers were of two types.

Access to goods and services

Many members argued that the current scale of LETS prevented anything more than occasional trading because the goods and services that could be accessed through LETS were limited. As one member put it:

"The LETS has never got to a sufficient scale, it hasn't achieved a 'critical mass'. I think that this has been the key problem. I've noticed that quite a few organisations have had a go but it just didn't work because it didn't get to the right size. So, it was sort of constrained a bit around the aromatherapy, massage market, which doesn't quite fit.... I mean it's just not going to be something that lots of people in Lambeth will want to join, it needs to be, well, not commercial exactly, but more based on sort of fundamental economic activity rather than sort of luxury services."

As this member highlights, it is not just the number of members that is an issue but also what they trade. In particular, a lack of formal business participation is seen to be restricting LETS development. One reason it is difficult for businesses to participate is because they end up with large credits that they find difficult to spend. Members dealt with this in different ways. Some stopped accepting LETS work and focused on spending local currency, for example:

"I've just had to stop doing work for others through LETS at the moment. I've built up around five hundred quid's worth of LETS, doing smallish building jobs, and I am just slowly spending it. You know, you can go for months without spending anything [in local currency], but you have to be able to find something to do with them. You've got to be able to spend them effectively, so at times it does get difficult. So I just withdraw for a while and focus on spending them."

Others unable to find ways to spend their large credits withdraw altogether.

"It's disappointing, I've been busy on the LETS providing garden design amongst other things, but I'm not actively trading anymore, and a lot of my friends in the LETS are of the same opinion. By that I mean they've got the same sort of reservations that I do, that they're building up quite a bit of credit but they're not getting what they want back. I'll renew my membership because I want to be part of it and I support the idea, but I'm not going to actively trade."

Circulation of goods and services

Members also found that the market was limited in terms of the length of time it took between deciding to offer a good or service, it being advertised and,

finally, someone responding to that offer. As members described:

"The speed of circulation in the LETS market – especially in second-hand goods – is really frustrating. When you want to sell something you want to sell it. So, my sofa, I had to wait a month before it went into the newsletter to be advertised. It's just not fast enough."

"The other problem was when you list your 'wants' you want them now. Well, we had a broken washing machine and wanted a plumber or someone and so it was put in, but by the time the directory was published, those things had been resolved. So things like that seem a bit of a waste of time – it's just not efficient."

Conclusions

The barriers to trading discussed in this chapter reveal some similarities with previous studies. Pearce and Wadhams (1998) note the constraints of the limited size of LETS on trading and its particular impact on key traders. Barnes et al (1996) also identify that a shortage of people willing or able to commit themselves to LETS organisation, and difficulties in negotiating prices, are barriers to advancement. However, our data also highlight some issues that have not been identified in the existing literature. These include:

- tensions surrounding the visibility of LETS;
- core group 'burnout';
- the transience of urban populations;
- the speed of circulation.

Furthermore, the case studies of Stroud and Brixton LETS, which are both long-standing schemes, indicate the importance of developing the organisational capacity of LETS if trading is to increase.

In sum, Chapters 10 and 11 have shown that both members and non-members identify a number of barriers to participation in LETS. Both groups challenge the notion of a "new discourse of debit" being created through LETS (Thorne, 1996). Not only do non-members have difficulty with this idea, but schemes themselves also seem unable to implement it in a practical day-to-day context, often reinforcing a notion of debt as negative by imposing limits on the amount of debit members could owe. Another set of barriers highlighted by these data surround skill identification and the pricing of work. It should be noted, however, that some members – typically those who are self-employed and therefore used to negotiating trades – did not find this problematic (see Aldridge et al, 2001: forthcoming). Members and non-members also questioned what they could receive through LETS and wanted guarantees about the quality of goods and services. This highlights a wider issue concerning the unregulated nature of LETS, which reinforced doubts about the credibility of schemes. This lack of credibility has been further exacerbated by the failure of LETS to attract significant levels of business participation, and this was the case despite the longevity of the schemes studied in depth. It is clear, therefore, that many of the barriers identified are overlapping. This poses a challenge for LETS aiming to develop beyond small-scale informal organisations. In Chapter 12 we highlight examples of strategies that individual LETS have adopted to tackle some of these barriers and, using data drawn from interviewing key figures in UK LETS development, we forward a series of recommendations that will be important for UK LETS development.

Part Five

Strategies for LETS development

12

Scaling LETS development: local, regional and national strategies

This chapter explores strategies for developing LETS at local, regional and national scales. It highlights examples of good practice and suggests some new ways to move forward. To explore these developmental issues, we take, in turn, the local, regional and national scales, and identify specific issues that need to be addressed if LETS are to be a more effective means of gaining access to work. Table 6 presents a summary of the strategies explored in this chapter.

Local strategies

At the local level of individual LETS, there are three key development issues that require attention if LETS are to become effective routes into work.

Publicity and marketing

As was shown in Chapter 10, many non-members had not heard of LETS. Clearly, therefore, a key problem is how LETS are currently publicised.

Accessibility

In earlier research, Barnes et al (1996) highlighted that the language used in promotional material did not reflect local knowledge and experience. While this was pronounced during the early phases of UK LETS development (when promotional materials discussed LETS as 'personal money'), notable examples of LETS exist which have produced high quality publicity materials that are accessible to wide audiences. For example, LETS developed in the London Borough of Greenwich, supported by the local authority, have been very successful in producing, not only brochures of a high quality

Table 6: Local, regional and national strategies to facilitate LETS development

Scale	Type of strategy	Changes required
Local	Organisational	Publicity and marketing – quality of publicity materials, targeting audiences and developing specific materials.
		Organisational capacity – increasing trading, creating links with other social economy initiatives, local authorities, businesses and community and voluntary groups.
		Regulating LETS – community chests, ensuring standards.
Regional	Organisational	Promotion and support of regional LETS networks – disseminating good practice, organising relevant training.
National	Institutional	Funding for national LETS development and promotion.
	Legislative	Changes required in benefit regulations concerning LETS earnings.

Adapted from: Aldridge and Patterson (2001)

which give LETS credibility, but materials that are also accessible to a range of people. For example, symbols have been used to represent trades to enable people with learning difficulties to use LETS directories more easily. While these materials have been disseminated to other LETS via conferences and workshops, a lack of funding and institutional 'thinness' at the regional or national level restricts more effective translation of this good practice. Resources need to be made available for disseminating useful promotional materials (for example, via the internet), providing training on how to create effective promotional materials and/or making a range of promotional technologies accessible to LETS. This could be enabled by greater partnership working with businesses and local authorities.

Visibility

In Stroud, LETS members also discussed the desire to establish a recognisable logo for LETS that could be promoted regionally and/or nationally. The aim was to increase visibility (for example by displaying the logo in windows of shops which accept LETS), to develop awareness and to enhance the legitimacy of LETS. However, given the limited resources available to most LETS, 'word-of-mouth' tends to be the principal means of promotion. For many, there is quite simply not enough money available to consider such publicity strategies.

Identifying groups and designing publicity to specific groups

It is not just the 'quality' of the publicity materials available but also the current marketing of LETS that needs to be developed. In Chapter 10, we drew attention to how non-members often felt that LETS publicity is aimed at a specific community. If the membership profile of LETS is to broaden, targeted marketing materials aimed at specific social groups must be developed. This requires identifying groups (for example, single parents, disabled people, unemployed people) and then providing examples of what existing members from these groups have offered and received on LETS. If undertaken, this would provide specific groups with more tailored information on what they could expect if they joined and participated in LETS. Such a strategy has been effectively implemented in some LETS funded by

local authorities (for example, Leicester), but these examples tend to remain at the local level. Again, greater networking at both regional and national levels could increase the effectiveness of such strategies.

Outreach work to expand membership

In addition to designing more appropriate publicity materials, there is also a need to engage in outreach work. Indeed, some local authorities (Greenwich, Liverpool, Leicester) have supported community development workers to do outreach work to raise awareness of LETS in order to extend membership to people on low incomes. The fact that local authorities support these LETS is important. This study has shown that LETS receiving financial support had more representative membership profiles. This indicates that funding is required to enable the marketing material and outreach work needed to broaden the membership base of LETS to a wider range of social groups. If the current strategy of 'word-of-mouth' remains dominant, the membership profile will remain skewed towards the specific social groups who have historically tended to join LETS.

Capacity building

There is also much good practice on capacity building and empowerment work that could be translated by community development workers. This is disseminated at conferences and seminars. However, many LETS are not able to participate in conferences given the limited resources in terms of time and money, and LETS need to be able to access such resources as and when required during development work. Thus, a funded national agency is required to collate information on this good practice and distribute it to local LETS.

Organisational capacity

Organisational capacity is a real problem, with directories becoming out-of-date, core group burnout and a lack of visibility. LETS also suffer a widespread lack of office space, equipment and training.

Financial support

The benefit of supporting organisational capacity financially is illustrated by the finding that the average level of trade per member was 27% higher in funded LETS. Furthermore, when groups receive funding, more time and energy becomes available to do necessary outreach work to develop the LETS. As we saw in Chapter 11, the small scale of LETS can be an issue in terms of the goods and services that can be purchased.

Increasing trading

As well as increasing the number of members, some LETS have developed innovative strategies for increasing trading. The example of Stirling and Alloa LETS is an important example of a LETS that has developed a number of strategies for increasing trade:

- The 'LETS make it better' (LMIB) project within Stirling and Alloa LETS, promotes the use of LETS for people with mental health problems. First, a standard hourly rate for all LETS work is used to reduce the problems of negotiating prices and to avoid the inequalities of the formal economy entering the pricing of LETS work – an issue that was identified as vitally important for people with mental health problems who are often excluded from formal employment.
- Also, gardening and maintenance 'gangs' have been developed. This 'team working' allows larger jobs to be undertaken solely for local currency and it gives people flexibility – if they are not able to do work on a particular day then the responsibility to complete the task is shared by the group. In addition, this strategy of working collectively in mixed groups, reduces the stigma felt by people with mental health problems being labelled by their illness and promotes greater interaction between LETS members. This greater interaction often results in higher levels of trading as people discuss work required and identify skills for completing these tasks.
- The success of the LMIB project in Stirling has led to a LETS café being developed. Initially, it was a drop-in café servicing LETS members and people using the community centre in which it was based. However, over time it has developed into a café in which LETS members have been trained to produce hot and cold buffets for local businesses.

Thus, the number of workers needed for its operation has increased, as has the range of skills that people are able to acquire through work in the café (see Manley and Aldridge, 2000).

Another strategy that LETS might use to increase trading is the creation of links with other local social economy initiatives, such as farmers' markets, credit unions and Time Money schemes. It is also necessary to examine ways for local authorities to trade in local currency, rather than solely to provide funding, and to explore how LETS can be promoted to local businesses and partnerships be developed with local community and voluntary organisations. These strategies could increase the size of the markets using local currency *and* reduce publicity and marketing costs by the joint promotion of schemes within the local area.

More innovative solutions include linking LETS development to the expanding services being piloted in rural Post Offices, such as those in rural Leicestershire. An idea would be to test using the Post Office as a 'bank' for LETS, so reinforcing the commitment made in the Rural White Paper of "ensuring that new initiatives are piloted in rural areas" (DETR/MAFF, 2000, p 37).

Regulating LETS

Typically, LETS are informally regulated. However, issues surrounding qualifications and quality have led some groups to consider more formal regulation.

Managing local currency

Many LETS currently adopt credit and debit limits to try to keep the system balanced. However, as we have highlighted above, with these in place, some people find the concept of debt problematic. In response to this, some LETS have developed a 'community chest'. Local currency is donated to this account which can then be distributed to those that need it. In Stroud this was discussed as a strategy for encouraging older people to participate. Given older people's reticence about going into debt, Stroud LETS members aimed to involve older people by offering them an amount of local currency to draw from to get them started. Conversely, effective incentives to trade such as progressive devaluation of credits may increase monetary credibility, although actions designed to reduce debt would undermine a fundamental tenet of LETS.

Standards of work

LETS are also beginning to put in place ways of ensuring standards of work. This is usually achieved by asking for information on qualifications to be published in the LETS directory. Other strategies include publicising recommendations of work in LETS newsletters. In addition, some groups have debated the idea of police checks for new members although to date this has not occurred. LETS in the London Borough of Greenwich have introduced the use of ID cards and passwords to ensure greater security.

Regional strategies

Currently, individual LETS operate on a fairly autonomous basis, but strategies developed at the regional scale could be a useful way to increase trading and membership. On a regional basis, LETS groups could meet regularly to share good practice and develop strategies at a far lower cost than national meetings.

Regional networks

At present, however, there are only a few regional networks. One example is Bristol and the surrounding region, which not only shares information, but also organises trading between groups. Another is a loose alliance of LETS groups across South West England which organises conferences. An even larger scale organisation is LETSLink Scotland that arranges conferences, seminars, workshops and newsletters.

National strategies

At the national level, two types of change are required in order to make LETS more effective bridges into work: institutional and legislative.

Institutional

At the national level, the coordinating agency is LETSLink UK. The agency started in 1991 with no

funding and was reliant on volunteers. LETSLink UK established a database of UK LETS and, for many years, dealt with the increasing number of enquiries about LETS. In addition, workers promoted LETS to the press – local, national and international, compiled a range of practical promotional materials (including a starter pack that has been used by many LETS), and produced a magazine on UK LETS development. During the 1990s, other organisations also emerged to develop LETS. These include: the LETSystem Trust; LETSGo; LETS Solutions; the Local Authority LETS Information Exchange (LALIE); and LETS Talk. In 1998, LETSLink UK received National Lottery funding to promote LETS development but subsequently lost this support leaving a vacuum at the national level. Other organisations have attempted to continue their development work but there remains a gap.

Thus, for LETS development to continue, there is a need for some form of funded national organisation that can act as a 'one-stop shop' for queries concerning LETS and as a provider of training packages. It is perhaps the LALIE that currently provides the most appropriate organisation for national-level promotion and advice. At present, however, it does not have a full- or even part-time worker but rather, is organised on a voluntary basis by local government officers. The funding of a full- or part-time post would provide the necessary resources to create this 'one-stop shop' for LETS and fill the void that currently exists at the national level.

Legislative

As identified in this study, the continued lack of clarity by central government about how LETS earnings will be treated with regard to benefits and taxation remains an important issue. Consequently, this research endorses the current policy proposal of the SEU (1998) for a pilot study to give people new freedom to earn a little casual income or participate in a Local Exchange and Trading Scheme (LETS) without affecting their benefit entitlement. Our research, however, shows that this policy shift alone is insufficient to encourage the wider participation of people on low incomes. There also needs to be changes in the amount that LETS participants can earn. Presently, it appears that the intention is to allow members to earn only up to the 'earnings disregard' before their benefits are reduced (DfEE,

1999). This study of LETS, however, suggests that, because LETS earnings are sporadic, flexibility is required with regard to the maximum weekly amounts people can earn. One option is to shift the weekly earnings disregard to an annual disregard limit.

Finally, some thought needs to be given to those who are coordinators of LETS. The change in the earnings disregard does little to recognise and value their work. And, if they are unemployed, it does not allay their fears that they may be considered 'not available for work'. This might be overcome to some extent by enabling such social entrepreneurship to be undertaken under the 'voluntary and community sector' of New Deal. Consideration might also be given to whether a greater proportion of these posts should be funded. However, if these suggestions are taken forward, the effectiveness of LETS cannot and should not be judged solely in terms of the number of jobs created. Alternative evaluation criteria are required, such as the number of trades conducted, the amount spent by members on skills acquisition and/ or the level of trade conducted by registered unemployed members.

Moreover, if LETS are to be pursued solely as a route into employment, the conventional job-related criteria discussed above can continue to be used. However, if they are treated more as a tool for providing a complementary means of livelihood, assessment needs to move beyond employment-related criteria towards alternative measures, such as the number of members and the spread of trading beyond the relatively small number of committed participants.

Conclusions

Most, if not all, of the development strategies for LETS discussed in this chapter involve increased levels of formalisation of one sort or another. This raises two critical issues. The first is:

* Is it worth it? What would be the benefit of trying to make LETS more effective?

Evidence presented in earlier chapters reveals the diverse and informal ways in which LETS are able to enhance the ability of people to earn a living and so

engage in social reproduction. This is due, in part, to the informality of LETS and to the facts that they are complex performative and practical institutions not limited to single issues. Rather, they address, and are capable of addressing, the complex and open-ended range of practices associated with social reproduction and earning a living. Any reform must, therefore, serve to enhance and not diminish this quality of LETS. If the development of LETS can achieve this objective, it is most definitely worth it.

However, the second issue cuts across the first:

* Would developmental strategies so transform LETS that their accessibility and character are changed?

In other words, does formalisation reduce the open-ended nature of LETS which is derived largely from their 'bottom-up' origins? LETS reflect local and often spontaneous and constructive responses to unacceptable circumstances. They are, therefore, self-motivated and locally directed. Developmental strategies almost inevitably transform these characteristics, so converting LETS into something other than institutions attractive to, and capable of, coping with the needs of local people locally expressed and experienced. The inevitable conclusion may be, therefore, that LETS schemes are faced with an inherent contradiction. Their attractiveness and effectiveness is based on their informality and spontaneity, but these characteristics also underpin the many barriers to joining and to trading identified in this report.

13

Summary and conclusions

This first comprehensive evaluation of LETS in the UK has revealed that, by 1999, some 303 LETS were operating. With an average of 72 members and a mean turnover equivalent to £4,664 per annum, the total UK LETS membership can be estimated at approximately 21,816, and the total annual turnover equivalent to some £1.4 million. In terms of their material contribution to social reproduction, these schemes are relatively insignificant compared with the wider economy. However, as with any economic system, their wider social contribution cannot be reduced to the sum of their flows of material value.

LETS members are predominantly aged 30-59, women, earning relatively low incomes and either not employed or self-employed. Indeed, if non-employment and low household income are taken as surrogate indicators of social exclusion, membership is heavily skewed towards socially excluded groups. Members, however, are predominantly from a particular group of the 'socially excluded' who tend to be well educated, to have few kinship networks in the locality and to be 'green' in political orientation. Indeed, in some cases, their 'exclusion' from mainstream employment appears to be due to their disenchantment with formal employment and a desire to build alternative forms of work and welfare.

Thus, in terms of why people join, a quarter does so for ideological purposes. LETS for them are 'expressive communities': acts of political protest and resistance to the 'mainstream', where ideals can be put into practice. Some 3%, however, join explicitly to improve their employability. A further quarter joins LETS as a 'social' vehicle for building communities, meeting people or helping others; and about half view them as an 'economic' vehicle for overcoming their lack of money, exchanging goods and services, using skills and receiving a specific service. 'Social' or community-building reasons tend to be cited by the employed and relatively affluent, and economic reasons by the relatively poor and unemployed.

Evaluating whether these members are currently able to use LETS as an effective bridge into work, this study has shown that, although LETS are moderately successful at maintaining and improving employability, they are more effective at providing a seed-bed for self-employed business ventures, and most successful at providing reciprocal exchange networks. On the issue of providing a route into employment, this study finds that, although just 5% of respondents said that LETS had *directly* helped them gain formal employment, many more said that they had *indirectly* provided them with a route into paid employment. Some 27% of all respondents asserted that the LETS had boosted their self-confidence (33% of the registered unemployed respondents) and 15% had acquired new skills through LETS (24% of the registered unemployed respondents) – mostly related to computing, administration and interpersonal skills.

If LETS contribute only indirectly to providing routes into employment, the same cannot be said of their role as facilitators of self-employment and alternative means of livelihood. Examining LETS as bridges into *self*-employment, this study has found that some 11% of members asserted that LETS had provided them with a useful testing ground for developing their self-employed business ventures. LETS had enabled them to develop their client base (cited by 41% of those who were self-employed), ease the cash-flow of their business (cited by 29%) and provide a test bed for their products and services (cited by nearly all who defined themselves as self-employed). Thus, although not a direct job creator, LETS do provide a useful springboard into employment and self-employment for a small but significant proportion of members.

However, the major contribution of LETS as a bridge into work is as a facilitator of reciprocal exchange. Some 76% of respondents asserted that LETS had helped them to develop a network of people on whom they could call for help, while 56% asserted that it had helped them develop a wider network of friends, and 31% deeper friendships. LETS, therefore, develop 'bridges' (that is, they bring people together who did not know each other before) more than 'bonds' (that is, bringing people who already know each other closer together). They develop the 'strength of weak ties' (Granovetter, 1973). For two thirds (65%) of the registered unemployed respondents, this had helped them cope with unemployment, with some 3% of their total income coming from their LETS activity. LETS are thus widely seen by members as an effective vehicle for developing means of livelihood beyond employment.

LETS thus represent a fascinating case study of how to construct bridges into work. However, this is not because they are effective at providing people with routes into employment but because they bring into focus the whole issue of what is meant by work and inclusion in contemporary society. Until recently, there has been a tendency in employment-centred social policy to assume that social inclusion can be equated with insertion into employment and that social exclusion can be equated with unemployment. LETS, however, reveal that there are many forms of inclusion and exclusion beyond employment and that there are many ways to tackle exclusion other than by simply trying to place people into jobs. By providing participants with the opportunity to forge coping practices beyond employment and illustrating that it is possible to harness one-to-one reciprocal exchange in contemporary society, LETS provide us with a demonstration that social reproduction is perfectly possible beyond formal employment. Indeed, in an age in which there are few other projects that demonstrate this possibility, LETS provide a pointer to the dangers inherent in a 'mono-economic' policy regime that focuses only on developing work conducted under the social relations of employment. Although the contemporary policy basket of formal employment creation is so dominant, LETS are one of the few vehicles that enable the development of work beyond employment. Although the contemporary policy basket of formal employment creation is so dominant, LETS are one of the few

vehicles that enable the development of work beyond employment.

Why, therefore, have so few people joined LETS? And why are trading levels so low on many LETS? This study has identified that significant barriers prevent a wider proportion of the population from participating. First, LETS currently cover only a limited area of the UK. Second, many people in the case study areas had never heard of them. Third, many potential members see LETS as something for people other than for them. Fourth, many people have little idea what they could contribute and, finally, the unemployed are fearful of how central government will react to their activity.

Our evidence suggests that LETS do offer a range of complex and very positive experiences. If these experiences are to be extended, a number of strategies might be employed. First, LETS might be developed where they do not exist. Second, awareness of their existence needs to be raised. Third, they need to be developed and promoted in inclusive rather than exclusive ways. Fourth, people need assistance to recognise their skills and talents and, last but not least, central governmental regulations need to be addressed. Our conclusion, therefore, is that these effective bridges into work will not suddenly blossom if a laissez-faire approach is adopted towards them, nor even by simply changing the benefit regulations to allow the unemployed to participate in them without fear of recrimination. Much more consideration will need to be given to the other barriers to participation if these bridges into work are to become of wider significance.

However, it is perhaps only by recognising the extent to which employment is now viewed as the only form of 'real' work and thinking afresh about how we want work and welfare to be structured in the future, that new bridges into work will be designed and implemented. Indeed, there is much to be learnt from LETS members who are using this initiative as a complementary means of social inclusion *beyond* employment rather than as a vehicle for helping them into formal employment. It is this complex refiguring of economic life within LETS which underpins the inherent contradiction between increasing their effectiveness through formalisation and facilitating them via the spontaneity and bottom-up creativity that have characterised their development to date.

References

Aldridge, T. and Patterson, A. (2001) 'LETS get real: examining the constraints to LETS development', Paper presented at the Annual RGS/IBG Conference, Alternative Economic Spaces Session, Plymouth 3-5 January.

Aldridge, T., Tooke, J., Lee, R., Leyshon, A., Thrift, N.J. and Williams, C.C. (2001: forthcoming) 'Recasting work: the example of Local Exchange Trading Schemes', *Work, Employment & Society*, vol 15.

Amin, A., Cameron, A. and Hudson, R. (1999) 'Welfare as work? The potential of the UK social economy', *Environment and Planning A*, vol 31, pp 2033-51.

Archibugi, F. (2000) *The associative economy: Insights beyond the welfare state and into post-capitalism*, London: Macmillan.

Barnes, H., North, P. and Walker, P. (1996) *LETS and low income*, London: The New Economics Foundation.

Barry, J. and Proops, J. (2000) *Citizenship, sustainability and environmental research: Q methodology and Local Exchange Trading Systems*, Cheltenham: Edward Elgar.

Beck, U. (2000) *The brave new world of work*, Cambridge: Polity Press.

Bennett, F. and Walker, R. (1998) *Working with work: An initial assessment of welfare to work*, York: Joseph Rowntree Foundation.

Bowring, F. (1998) 'LETS: an eco-socialist initiative?', *New Left Review*, vol 232, pp 91-111.

Boyle, D. (1999) *Funny money: In search of alternative cash*, London: Harper Collins.

Button, K. (1984) 'Regional variations in the irregular economy: a study of possible trends', *Regional Studies*, vol 18, pp 385-92.

Cannon, D. (1994) *Generation X and the new work ethic*, London: Demos.

Catterall, B., Lipietz, A., Hutton, W. and Girardet, H. (1996) 'The third sector, urban regeneration and the stakeholder society', *City*, nos 5-6, pp 86-102.

CDF (Community Development Foundation) (1995) *Added value and changing values: community involvement in urban regeneration: a 12 country study for the European Union*, final report, CEC DG XVI.

Chanan, G. (1999) 'Employment and the third sector: promise and misconceptions', *Local Economy*, vol 13, pp 361-8.

Coupland, D. (1991), *Generation X: Tales for an accelerated culture*, New York, NY: St Martin's Press.

Croall, J. (1997) *LETS act locally: The growth of Local Exchange Trading Systems*, London: Calouste Gulbenkian Foundation.

Dauncey, G. (1996) *After the crash: The emergence of the rainbow economy*, London: Greenprint.

DETR (Department of the Environment, Transport and the Regions) (1998) *Community-based regeneration initiatives: A working paper*, London: DETR.

DETR (1999) *Community enterprise: Good practice guide*, London: DETR.

DETR/MAFF (Ministry of Agriculture, Fisheries and Food) (2000) *Our countryside: The future – a fair deal for rural England*, Cmnd 4909, London: DETR.

DfEE (Department for Education and Employment) (1999) *Jobs for all: National strategy for neighbourhood renewal: PAT 1*, Nottingham: DfEE.

Dobson, R.V.G. (1993) *Bringing the economy home from the market*, New York, NY: Black Rose Books.

Douthwaite, R. (1996) *Short circuit: Strengthening local economies for security in an uncertain world*, Dartington: Green Books.

DSS (Department of Social Security) (1999) *Opportunity for all: Tackling poverty and social exclusion*, Cmnd 4445, London: HMSO.

Dunford, M. (1997) 'Diversity, instability and exclusion: regional dynamics in Great Britain', in R. Lee and J. Wills (eds) *Geographies of Economies*, London: Arnold.

ECOTEC (1998) *Third system and employment: Evaluation inception report*, Birmingham: ECOTEC.

Engbersen, G., Schuytt, K., Timmer, J. and van Waarden, F. (1993) *Cultures of unemployment: A comparative look at long-term unemployment and urban poverty*, Oxford: Westview.

European Commission (1996) *Social and economic inclusion through regional development: The community economic development priority in ESF programmes in Great Britain*, Brussels: European Commission.

European Commission (1997) *Towards an urban agenda in the European Union*, Communication from the European Commission COM (97), 197, Brussels: European Commission.

European Commission (1998) *The era of tailor-made jobs: second report on local development and employment initiatives*, Brussels: European Commission.

Evers, A. and Wintersberger, H. (eds) (1988) *Shifts in the welfare mix: Their impact on work, social services and welfare policies*, Vienna: European Centre for Social Welfare Training and Research.

Fitzpatrick, T. and Caldwell, C. (2001: forthcoming) 'Towards a theory of ecosocial welfare: radical reformism and local exchange and trading systems', in T. Fitzpatrick and M. Cahill (eds) *Greening the welfare state*, Basingstoke: Palgrave.

Fordham, G. (1995) *Made to last: Creating sustainable neighbourhood and estate regeneration*, York: Joseph Rowntree Foundation.

Giddens, A. (1998) *The third way: The renewal of social democracy*, Cambridge: Polity Press.

Giddens, A. (2000) *The third way and its critics*, Cambridge: Polity Press.

Gorz, A. (1999) *Reclaiming work: Beyond wage-based society*, Cambridge: Polity Press.

Granovetter, M. (1973) 'The strength of weak ties', *American Journal of Sociology*, vol 78, pp 1360-80.

Greco, T.H. (1994) *New money for healthy communities*, Tucson, AZ: Greco.

Gregg, P. and Wadsworth, J. (1996) *It takes two: Employment polarisation in the OECD*, Discussion Paper No 304, London: Centre for Economic Performance, London School of Economics and Political Science.

Gregg, P., Johnson, P. and Reed, H. (1999) *Entering work and the British tax and benefit system*, London: Institute for Fiscal Studies.

Gregory, A. and Windebank, J. (2000) *Women's work in Britain and France: Theory, practice and policy*, Basingstoke: Macmillan.

Gutmann, P.M. (1978) 'Are the unemployed, unemployed?', *Financial Analysts Journal*, vol 35, pp 26-7.

Habermas, J. (1975) *Legitimation crisis*, London: Heinemann.

Hart, K. (2000) *The memory bank: Money in an unequal world*, London: Profile Books.

Haughton, G. (1998) 'Principles and practice of community economic development', *Regional Studies*, vol 32, pp 872-8.

Hetherington, K. (1998) *Expressions of identity: Space, performance, politics*, London: Sage Publications.

Hills, J. (1998) *Thatcherism, New Labour and the welfare state*, CASE Paper 13, London: Centre for the Analysis of Social Exclusion, London School of Economics and Political Science.

HM Treasury (1997) *Employment opportunity in a changing labour market*, London: HM Treasury.

HM Treasury (1998) *The modernisation of Britain's tax and benefit system: The Working Families Tax Credit and work incentives*, London: HM Treasury.

Home Office (1999) *Community self-help: PAT 9*, London: Home Office.

Jordan, B. (1998) *The new politics of welfare: Social justice in a global context*, London: Sage Publications.

Jordan, B., Agulnik, P., Burbridge, D. and Duffin, S. (2000) *Stumbling towards basic income: The prospects for tax-benefit integration*, London: Citizen's Income Study Centre.

Komter, A.E. (1996) 'Reciprocity as a principle of exclusion: gift giving in the Netherlands', *Sociology*, vol 30, pp 299-316.

Kropotkin, P. (1902) *Mutual aid: A factor in evolution*, London: Porter Sargent.

Lang, P. (1994) *LETS work: Revitalising the local economy*, Bristol: Grover.

Lee, R. (1996) 'Moral money? LETS and the social construction of economic geographies in south east England', *Environment and Planning A*, vol 28, pp 1377-94.

Lee, R., Leyshon, A., Aldridge, T., Thrift, N.J., Tooke, T. and Williams, C.C. (2000) 'Constructing alternative circuits of value: the case of local currency systems', Paper presented at International Geographical Union Study Group on Local Development Annual Conference, 'The Institutions of Local Development', Trento, Italy, 19-21 October.

Leonard, M. (1998) *Invisible work, invisible workers: The informal economy in Europe and the US*, Basingstoke: Macmillan.

Levitas, R. (1998) *The inclusive society? Social exclusion and New Labour*, Basingstoke: Macmillan.

Lietaer, B. (2001) *The future of money*, London: Random House.

Linton M, (1986) 'Local currency', in P. Ekins (ed) *The living economy: A new economics in the making*, London: Routledge and Kegan Paul, pp 196-203.

Lister, R. (1997) *Citizenship: Feminist perspectives*, Basingstoke: Macmillan.

Macfarlane, R. (1996) *Unshackling the poor: A complementary approach to local economic development*, York: Joseph Rowntree Foundation.

Manley, C. and Aldridge, T. (2000) 'Can LETS make it better? A Stirling example', *A Life in the Day*, vol 4, no 4, pp 2-9.

Matthews, K. (1983) 'National income and the black economy', *Journal of Economic Affairs*, vol 3, pp 261-67.

Mayer, M. and Katz, S. (1985) 'Gimme shelter: self-help housing struggles within and against the state in New York City and West Berlin', *International Journal of Urban and Regional Research*, vol 9, pp 123-56.

Mayo, E. (1996) 'Dreaming of work', in P. Meadows (ed) *Work out or work in? Contributions to the debate on the future of work*, York: Joseph Rowntree Foundation, pp 47-57.

North, P. (1996) 'LETS: a tool for empowerment in the inner city?', *Local Economy*, vol 11, pp 284-93.

North, P. (1998) 'Exploring the politics of social movements through "sociological intervention": a case study of Local Exchange Trading Schemes', *Sociological Review*, vol 46, pp 564-82.

North, P. (1999) 'Explorations in heterotopia: LETS and the micropolitics of money and livelihood', *Environment and Planning D: Society and Space*, vol 17, pp 69-86.

O'Connor, J. (1973) *The fiscal crisis of the state*, London: St. Martin's Press.

O'Doherty, R.K., Durrschmidt, J., Jowers, P. and Purdue, D.A. (1999) 'Local exchange and trading schemes: a useful strand of community economic development policy?', *Environment and Planning A*, vol 31, pp 1639-53.

OECD (Organisation for Economic Cooperation and Development) (1995) *Trickle down or bubble up? The challenge of urban regeneration*, Paris: OECD.

OECD (1996) *Reconciling economy and society: Towards a plural economy*, Paris: OECD.

Offe, C. and Heinze, R.G. (1992) *Beyond employment: Time, work and the informal economy*, Cambridge: Polity Press.

Oppenheim, C. (1998) 'Welfare to work: taxes and benefits', in J. McCormick and C. Oppenheim (eds) *Welfare in working order*, London: Institute for Public Policy Research.

Pacione, M. (1997a) 'Local Exchange Trading Systems as a response to the globalisation of capitalism', *Urban Studies*, vol 34, pp 1179-99.

Pacione, M. (1997b) 'Local Exchange Trading Systems: a rural response to the globalisation of capitalism?', *Journal of Rural Studies*, vol 13, pp 415-27.

Pacione, M. (1997c) 'Toward a community economy: an examination of Local Exchange Trading Systems in Glasgow', *Urban Geography*, vol 19, pp 211-31.

Pahl, R.E. (1984) *Divisions of labour*, Oxford: Basil Blackwell.

Pahl, R.E. (1995) 'Finding time to live', *Demos*, vol 5, pp 12-13.

Pearce, J. and Wadhams, C. (1998) *Uncommon currencies: LETS and their impact on property repair and maintenance for low income homeowners*, Bristol/York: The Policy Press/Joseph Rowntree Foundation.

Pinch, S. (1993) 'Social polarisation: a comparison of evidence from Britain and the United States', *Environment and Planning A*, vol 25, pp 779-95.

Powell, M. (1999) 'Introduction', in M. Powell (ed) *New Labour, new welfare state: The 'third way' in British social policy*, Bristol: The Policy Press, pp 1-14.

Purdue, D.A., Durrschmidt, J., O'Doherty, R.K. and Jowers, P. (1997) 'DIY culture and extended milieux: LETS, veggie boxes and festivals', *Sociological Review*, vol 45, pp 645-67.

Putnam, R.D. (2000) *Bowling alone: The collapse and revival of American community*, New York, NY: Simon and Schuster.

Renooy, P. (1990) *The informal economy: Meaning, measurement and social significance*, Netherlands Geographical Studies No 115, Amsterdam.

Sen, A. (1998) *Inequality reexamined*, Oxford: Clarendon Press.

Seyfang, G. (1998) *Green money from the grassroots: Local exchange trading schemes and sustainable development*, Submitted PhD thesis, Leeds: Centre for Urban Development and Environmental Management, Leeds Metropolitan University.

Smiles, S. (1866) *Self-help: With illustrations of character, conduct and perseverance*, London: Murray.

SEU (Social Exclusion Unit) (1998) *Bringing Britain together: A national strategy for neighbourhood renewal*, London: Cabinet Office.

SEU (2000) *National strategy for neighbourhood renewal: A framework for consultation*, London: The Stationery Office.

Stringer, E.T. (1996) *Action research: A handbook for practitioners*, London: Sage Publications.

Thomas, J.J. (1992) *Informal economic activity*, Hemel Hempstead: Harvester Wheatsheaf.

Thorne, L. (1996) 'Local exchange trading systems in the United Kingdom: a case of re-embedding?', *Environment and Planning A*, vol 28, pp 1361-76.

Tibbett, R. (1997) 'Alternative currencies: a challenge to globalisation?', *New Political Economy*, vol 2, no 1, pp 127-35.

Urry, J. (2000) *Sociology beyond societies: Mobilities for the twenty-first century*, London: Routledge.

Westerdahl, S. and Westlund, H. (1998) 'Third sector and new jobs: a summary of twenty case studies in European regions', *Annals of Public and Co-operative Economics*, vol 69, pp 193-218.

Williams, C.C. (1996a) 'Local Exchange and Trading Systems (LETS): a new form of work and credit for the poor and unemployed', *Environment and Planning A*, vol 28, pp 1395-415.

Williams, C.C. (1996b) 'Informal sector responses to unemployment: an evaluation of the potential of Local Exchange and Trading Systems (LETS)', *Work, Employment & Society*, vol 10, pp 341-59.

Williams, C.C. (1996c) 'Local currencies and community development: an evaluation of green dollar exchanges in New Zealand', *Community Development Journal*, vol 31, pp 319-29.

Williams, C.C. (1997) 'Local Exchange and Trading Systems (LETS) in Australia: a new tool for community development', *International Journal of Community Currencies Research*, vol 1, pp 32-49.

Williams, C.C. (2001) 'Does work pay? Spatial variations in the benefits of employment and coping abilities of the unemployed', *Geoforum*, vol 32, no 2, pp 199-214.

Williams, C.C. and Windebank, J. (1995) 'Social polarisation of households in contemporary Britain: a "whole economy" perspective', *Regional Studies*, vol 29, pp 727-32.

Williams, C.C. and Windebank, J. (1999) *A helping hand: Harnessing self-help to combat social exclusion*, York: York Publishing Services.

Williams, C.C. and Windebank, J. (2000) 'Helping people to help themselves: policy lessons from a study of deprived urban neighbourhoods in Southampton', *Journal of Social Policy*, vol 29, pp 355-73.

Williams, C.C. and Windebank (2001a) 'Beyond social inclusion through employment: harnessing mutual aid as a complementary social inclusion policy', *Policy & Politics*, vol 29, no 1, pp 15-28.

Williams, C.C. and Windebank, J. (2001b) *Revitalising deprived urban neighbourhoods: An assisted self-help approach*, London: Ashgate.

Williams, C.C., White, R. and Aldridge, T. (2001) *Community self-help in rural England: Its role in tackling poverty and exclusion*, London: The Countryside Agency.

World Bank (1997) *World Development Report*, Oxford: Oxford University Press.

Yankelovich, D. (1995) *Young adult Europe*, Paris: Yankelovich Monitor.

Zoll, R. (1989) *Nicht so wie unsere Eltern*, Opladen: Westdeutscher Verlag.

Appendix A:
Case studies of LETS

Brixton LETS

Name of local currency: Bricks
Location: Inner London
Founded: January 1992
Origins: Set up by friends sharing a house who wished to create a 'green community-based economy'. Over time, the community-building and green economy foci have gradually given way to a greater emphasis on helping disadvantaged people.

Relationship of local currency to sterling: Floating
Debit limit: 250 bricks
Minimum wage rate: 5 bricks per hour

Total turnover: Equivalent of £35,000

Number of accounts: 170
including:
- 2 registered businesses (eg, art gallery)
- 4 community organisations (Brixton Common Land, Bannington Centre, Green Adventure and Ecotrip)
- 1 church

Trading: 20% of members trade more than 10 times each year, 60% between 5-10 times and 20% do not trade at all.

Membership profile: Although 55% of members are unwaged, this proportion is gradually declining as more employed people join the scheme. At present, the view of the LETS is that both non-white people and men are under-represented, and the perception is that people from ethnic minority communities in particular feel excluded from joining.

External funding (1999): None

Stroud LETS

Name of local currency: Strouds
Location: Small semi-rural town in South West England
Founded: January 1991
Origins: A group of people who saw it as a good idea for an 'alternative' small town.

Relationship of local currency to sterling: None
Debit limit: None
Minimum wage rate: None

Number of accounts: 350
including:
- 15 registered businesses (including 2 shops, 2 cafés)
- 2 community organisations (the local credit union, community shop)
- 5 voluntary organisations

Trading: 50% of members trade more than 10 times each year.

Membership profile: Although 71% of members are jobless, most of the membership is green in political orientation with some 60% supporting the Green Party.

External funding (1999): None

Appendix B:
Groups that participated in the non-member research in Stroud and Brixton

Stroud	Brixton
Job Club	Lambeth Women's Workshop Ltd.
Family Centre	Lambeth Pathways Employment Service
123 Parent and Toddlers Group	Community Support Network, Mental Health Management Committee
Stroud Friendly Circle – Pensioners Group	Foundation for Human Development
The Door Youth Project	NACRO – New Careers Training
Women's Refuge	Railton Road Methodist Church Group
Meals on Wheels Volunteer Group	Lambeth Unemployment Project
Gloucester Disability Forum	Lambeth Accord
Trinity Fellowship Church Group	Lambeth Crime Prevention Trust
	STFCH Housing Association, Stockwell Estate
	Brixton Society

Appendix C:
Web contacts for
LETS in the UK

LETS schemes

LETSLink UK .... http://www.letslinkuk.org
LETSLink Scotland .... http://www.letslinkscotland.org.uk
LETS in Wales .... http://www.teifitaf.freeserve.co.uk/cymru/cyfle.htm
LETSlink London .... http://www.oneworld.org/letslinklondon

LETSystems

LETSystems .... http://www.letsystems.net/word.cm
.... http://www.gmlets.u-net.com

E-mail discussion on LETS

Econ-lets .... http://www.jiscmail.ac.uk/lists/econ-lets.html

Research on LETS

International Journal of Community Currency Research .... http://www.geog.le.ac.uk/ijccr/
ESRC LETS project website .... http://www.geog.qmw.ac.uk/lets
LETS Talk – interactive newsletter on LETS .... http://nt.oneworld.org/lets

List of contacts for other related social economy initiatives

New Economics Foundation .... http://www.neweconomics.org
Local Interest Free Trading .... http://www.lift.ltd.uk
Fair Shares (UK pilot of the American Time Dollars system) .... http://www.fairshares.org.uk
UK time currencies .... http://www.timebanks.co.uk
Time currencies .... http://ourworld.compuserve.com/homepages/dcboyle
Time Dollar Institute .... http://www.timedollar.org
Social Enterprise London .... http://www.sel.org.uk/